Vanishing
Britain

Dysart, Fife

Other titles by Roy Christian

Old English Customs
Ghosts and Legends
The Peak District

Vanishing Britain

Roy Christian

Foreword by Christopher Hall, Director,
Council for the Protection of Rural England

David & Charles
Newton Abbot   London
North Pomfret (VT)   Vancouver

ISBN 0 7153 7346 3

Library of Congress Catalog Card Number
76–58790

Set in 10 on 11pt Plantin
and printed in Great Britain
by Biddles Limited, Guildford
for David & Charles (Publishers) Limited
Brunel House Newton Abbot Devon

Published in the United States of America
by David & Charles Inc
North Pomfret Vermont 05053 USA

Published in Canada
by Douglas David & Charles Limited
1875 Welch Street North Vancouver BC

Contents

Red squirrel

Foreword

I groaned when I read the title of this book. Another doom-laden farewell to the countryside and our historic towns and villages. I did not believe that on these well worn themes there could be anything new to say or any new perspective to be furnished.

I was wrong.

Roy Christian floats above the conservation battlefield like an old-time war correspondent in a balloon. Calmly retentive of civilised values while all beneath him is carnage, pad on knee he notes the ebb and flow of fortune below: here a victory for reason and sensitivity; there a defeat; there again a frustrating draw.

His is a geographically all-embracing view. One of the nicest things about Mr Christian's book is that you are bound to find in it mention of places you know or love and that mention you will at once recognise to be crisp and authoritative. He has a gift for catching the spirit of place.

To aid him in this capture Mr Christian has the resources of a well read mind to call upon. Of course he invokes Housman when discussing Shropshire. Less obviously he also invokes P. G. Wodehouse, and some of us believe that the latter understood Shropshire better than the former.

Richard Jeffries—a connoisseur's choice this—is cited in defence of hedgerows: 'Without hedges, England would not be England.' But I think Mr Christian is a little too optimistic about the future of hedges. Despite all the good intentions expressed by farmers and landowners, they are still disappearing at the rate of some 2,500 miles a year. Nothing but legislation is likely to check this vandalism.

I also suspect Mr Christian of showing a little favouritism to the East Midlands and East Anglia. And why not? Both are regions which are too often left out of account, so his emphasis on their charms is no bad thing.

What then emerges from this bird's eye—or balloonist's eye —view? In short, Mr Christian's belief that the forces of light are defeating the forces of darkness. A comforting message, though one of which Mr Christian is himself the first to say that it affords no ground for complacency.

Is he right? The answer is Yes and No. Yes—as far as the battles covered in this book are concerned. No, so far as some of the regional and national battles now looming are concerned.

Essentially Mr Christian's battlefield is the localised one, the kind of struggle in which the local civic or amenity society, the local council or even the dedicated individual can decide the issue. One of the most heartening things in the book is the stress he places on the role of people close to the problems they are tackling. My own favourite is his reference to Margaret Powell's one-woman crusade to save Beverley's gracious Lady-gate. I know Margaret Powell and I take her to be the archetype of the unassuming, determined and resourceful citizens who in recent years have fought so hard for our environment and our heritage.

But Mr Christian knows that conservation is about more than the preservation of the physical fabrics we admire. His comparison of three neighbouring Cotswold villages—Bourton-on-the-Water (sold out to commercialism), Lower Slaughter (so tidy you feel you must wipe your boots before entering) and Guiting Power (friendly and unselfconscious because it is being revived as a community for local people to live in)—is a telling one; and the lesson he draws from it is wholly in favour of the last of the three settlements.

Villages in Mr Christian's view are more than pretty-pretty conservation areas. They have—or should have—souls as well.

And what of the larger battlefield not comprehended within even Mr Christian's view? I am thinking of the rape of landscape and farmland by the still bloated roads programme. I am thinking of the grandiose blueprints of regional planners still disastrously hagridden by dreams of growth, growth and yet more growth.

It is no criticism of Mr Christian that he does not deal with these problems. He has given us a conspectus of his conservation battlefield at the moment when it has reached a certain clarity and there are lessons we can learn from his account which will help to guide us through the new battles ahead.

These new battles emerge naturally and logically from the strength and self-reliance which the conservation movement has discovered at local level, and which Mr Christian charts. We began by arguing about the route of a new road; now we are prepared to challenge the need for it at all, and better still, to try to cut down to size the roads programme of which it is a part. We began by querying the siting and size of a new estate. Now we challenge the regional plan, prepared in some remote and undemocratic 'economic planning council', which the speculative builder uses to justify it.

My hope is that Mr Christian will let his balloon drift over these battlefields too before long.

Christopher Hall,
Director of the Council for the Protection of Rural England

8

1 Going, Going...

The Seaboard—erosion and reclamation

The tower of an ancient church perched precariously halfway down a crumbling cliff and surrounded by rank grass out of which sprouted a crop of absurdly tilted headstones poised above a beach littered with more gravestones, some upright, others flat and licked clean by the advancing tide; such was my introduction to a vanishing Britain.

It is one of my earliest memories, that first visit to Dunwich. I suppose I must have been four or five and World War I was not long over. I can remember nothing else of the walk from Walberswick on what was probably our first family holiday after the war; certainly my first visit to Suffolk and the sea. When I went back there a few years ago, nothing remained of the ruined church. A single flat stone half embedded in sand could have been a gravestone, but was more likely a relic of a World War II gun emplacement.

Dunwich is just one place—perhaps the most famous—that the sea swallowed. More fortunate than some, it has retained 'a local habitation and a name', for in the nineteenth century a new village of Dunwich was built well back from the boulder clay cliffs and the site of the old town. Other places have vanished entirely; Shakespeare's Ravenser for one. Like Dunwich, it used to return two members of parliament in the Middle Ages. Close to Ravenser, on the Holderness coast between Bridlington and Spurn Head, in what is now the county of Humberside, 'several towns were formerly known to be there, which are now lost,' as Daniel Defoe put it more than 250 years ago. Auburn, Dimlington, Great Colden, Hartburn, Horton, Hyde . . . and a dozen or so more have gone from that stretch of coast. The sole survivor of 24 modern bungalows on the edge of the low cliff at Barmston seemed likely to join them at any moment when I was last there late in 1973. Further south, Fidesthorpe, Shipden, Snitterley and other places along the Norfolk seaboard have all been swept away, not in some violent tidal wave but gradually, over the years, through the slow process of coastal erosion.

Such gradual eating away of the low cliffs and dunes is caused by the force of waves made doubly lethal by a secondary armament of sharp rocks and pebbles that are debris from eroded cliffs, and sometimes helped by springs gushing from the cliff face. Gradually the base of the cliff is weakened, eventually worn away. Then the overhanging rocks collapse; the sea has won another victory.

Such victories may be won almost anywhere around the coasts of Britain, but they are gained most easily against the soft boulder clay cliffs of Holderness and East Anglia. The Holderness coast recedes by about $7\frac{1}{2}$ft a year. Since Roman times around 83 square miles of land there—roughly half the size of the old county of Rutland—have disappeared. In East Anglia the land recedes by 5–6ft annually. Further south, the Isle of Sheppey loses some $2\frac{1}{2}$ acres every year. Even the tougher cliffs of Dover do not stand unscathed, the Straits widening by about one foot a year.

It may sound as if Britain is shrinking, but in fact what the sea takes from one place it puts back in another. On the East Coast it usually deposits the detritus on the north side of some promontory such as Spurn Head, the northern tip of the Humber estuary, or Gibraltar Point, north of the Wash. Spurn's nothern side is indeed growing by about 9ft a year, and the Gibraltar Point coastguard station that is shown at the water's edge in the first—early nineteenth century—Ordnance Survey map of the area is now a mile from the sea.

In some places the normal processes of accretion and silting have been supplemented by civil engineers with their enclosing walls and pumping engines. A Royal Commission on Sea Erosion in 1911 estimated that 48,000 acres of new land had been added to Britain in the previous 35 years while only 680 acres had been lost. Since then the New Docks at Southampton and the oil refinery at Fawley have been built on reclaimed land, as have industrial sites on Teesside, while much land has been recovered from the Dee and Ribble estuaries and from Morecambe Bay. So while parts of Britain are vanishing under the sea—and the losses include houses as well as attractive scenery—we are literally more than making up the lost ground.

Problems of water storage

Where we are certainly not making up lost ground is in the land we are losing, not by what insurance people call 'acts of God', but by deliberate acts of man in his insatiable demand for water. Land drowned under reservoirs is irreplaceable, and except in hard economic terms there is no adequate compensation for people who lose their homes, farming land or favourite beauty spot.

Must we continue to lose land for water-storage purposes? Yes, we must, according to the 1974 report of the Water Resources Board—its last word before handing its work over to ten regional water authorities. In England and Wales alone we consume more than 3,000 million gallons of water a day and are likely to double our demands by the end of the century. As

we have not advanced far in our ability to desalinate water
from the sea, we must face the building of three new reservoirs
and the enlargement of another before 1981. Between then and
the end of the century two more reservoirs must be constructed,
and two existing ones enlarged. There is also a possibility that
the Dee estuary may be used for water storage.

It sounds a fairly reasonable sacrifice to make in order to slake
our national thirst, especially with the 1976 drought fresh in
our minds. Unfortunately, most of these reservoirs are likely
to be built in the hillier, wetter north and west of England or
in Wales. These are the natural gathering grounds for water;
they are also the natural gathering grounds for walkers, climbers
and those who just like to 'get away from it all' in what little
wilderness is left to us. There are those who argue that reservoirs
sometimes add beauty to otherwise barren scenes; others that
they provide opportunities for water sports. Both points have
some validity, but in fact, because of pollution dangers, sailing
and other aquatic activities are permitted on only a few new
reservoirs. As for the other argument, it is true that many like
to picnic beside these artificial lakes, but it is equally true that
the lover of solitude shuns them. They remind him of the
urban environment he seeks to escape. Reservoirs tame the
landscape. Just as it is more exciting to see wild animals in
their natural habitat than behind bars, so it is more exciting to

1 Unlike some reservoirs which
add a jarring note to wild scenery,
Ladybower, in the Peak District,
merges with the landscape

11

tramp across a virgin wilderness than across country where man has left his imprint in concrete dams and retaining walls.

Much of our remaining wilderness lies within the ten national parks. These are areas much sought after by water authorities. There are 51 reservoirs within the Peak District National Park and another 22 just outside in areas that may eventually be added to the park. If the Water Resources Board report leads to action a twenty-third may shortly be built at Carsington. Other national parks, notably Brecon, Dartmoor and the North Yorkshire Moors, have had unwanted reservoirs thrust upon them, with perhaps others to come, despite strong protests. The planners counter with the argument that as the parks cover about one-tenth of England and Wales and an even higher proportion of the most eligible gathering ground they can hardly expect to remain sacrosanct.

Not that all new reservoirs are built within the parks. As I write, water is gradually filling a reservoir at Empingham, in what used to be called Rutland, drowning 1,400 acres of attractive agricultural land. Another 400 acres of fertile Suffolk farmland, together with three listed buildings and numerous archaeological sites, will shortly disappear under Tattingstone Reservoir, or Alton Water, as the planners euphemistically call it.

But let us not be beastly to the planners. They have a necessary job to do and more often than not they do it considerately. This was exemplified in the row over Cow Green Reservoir, if 'row' is not too strong a term to describe what was generally a highly civilised attempt to reconcile the needs of Teesside—and particularly of ICI—with the needs of botanists to preserve an area of unique scientific interest.

In 1956 the Tees Valley and Cleveland Water Board chose Cow Green in the upper Tees Valley as a possible reservoir site, but changed its corporate mind on being warned of possible geological problems. Another site five miles downstream was abandoned after Nature Conservancy opposition, and eventually a reservoir was built at Balderhead. But even before this land was flooded the Board realised that an extra 23 million gallons of water a day would be needed to meet the requirements of Teesside industry by 1969–70. Nine sites were considered and rejected before the Board returned to Cow Green as the only site that could be used economically in time to save perhaps 50,000 jobs that could have been lost through a water shortage. Part of the area was in the Upper Teesdale National Nature Reserve, another portion was likely to be included and much of the rest was designated a Site of Special Scientific Interest, so there were strong objections from relevant conservationist bodies. Between 1964 and 1966 the opposing sides met frequently in attempts to reach a compromise, but eventually the Board had its way. An Act of Parliament for building the reservoir was passed in 1967. The reservoir is built now. Fortunately many of the rarer plants were transferred to other suitable sites before work started. But another precious bit of Britain vanished.

Mineral extraction

Lord Kennet, speaking from the chair, told the annual conference of the Council for the Protection of Rural England in 1971, 'If we go on as we are going now, the South East of England will be entirely covered with development in 200 years' time, and the whole of England in 300. This is a sober calculation, based on a projection of the best figures, including urban development, reservoirs, airfields, roads and so on. With the recently announced Government subsidies to stimulate mining in this country, most of which is going to be opencast mining, it may be that these figures are even optimistic.'

Lord Kennet's figures related to England only, but boundaries on a map are no protection against the rape of the countryside. In the pursuit of opencast coal, mechanical earth movers were tearing away 300 million tons of Britain's outer shell annually by 1975 and had dug a hole 1,000ft deep at Westfield in Fife, though elsewhere 400ft was usually the maximum depth. Fortunately, except for those who live there, most of this work is going ahead in areas already scarred by deep mining, but the National Coal Board will literally break fresh ground when work starts on coal extraction some 800–3,900ft beneath 110 square miles of good farming land between Selby and York. In the future the East Midland coalfield may spread eastward into Lincolnshire, a county so far only grazed by large-scale industrial exploitation. Already, the Coal Board plans to exploit the fertile Vale of Belvoir, astride the Nottinghamshire–Leicestershire border within 10 miles of Lincolnshire's western limits.

Other minerals lie beneath beautiful surfaces. More than 200,000 tons of fluorspar is extracted annually from the Peak District National Park by underground mining, opencast excavations and reworking old lead-mine spoil dumps. This is over 70 per cent of total British production. Much of the ore is crushed for use in the chemical industry in the two largest processing plants in Britain. One is in the National Park at Stoney Middleton, the other just outside at Hopton. Both are unsightly as are the large slimey lakes called tailing lagoons into which the waste material is pumped. But if the fluorspar industry diminishes the attractions of the Peak, its products add, at 1974 prices, about £3 million annually to Britain's export earnings. Attractive scenery, unfortunately, issues no balance sheet.

Within the national parks even greater wealth comes—and greater mess is left behind—by quarrying, especially for limestone. Limestone quarrying not only opens up ugly wounds on hillsides but also spreads frosty films of dust over surrounding trees and hedges and in neighbouring watercourses, generates noise and smoke and creates traffic hazards by releasing stone-filled lorries into roads not always adequate to cope with horses and carts.

Nobody would want to stop limestone quarrying entirely. Limestone is needed by the iron, steel, chemical and cement industries, as well as for aggregates—especially for roadstone, for which suitable alternatives could surely be found. Quarrying, though not a labour intensive industry, is also the main source of employment in some areas. And what price beauty when the value of limestone in Mendip was estimated at about £30,000 million at 1972 prices? In the face of such a figure it was courageous of the National Trust to close a small quarry on their property in Borrowdale because the scale of the workings was becoming objectionable. Equally commendable was the decision of the Peak Park Planning Board in 1974 to refuse planning permission to ICI to extend their Tunstead Quarry, the largest in Europe, into the park, even though the refusal may amount to no more than a temporary stay of execution.

Meanwhile large swaths of land, especially in river valleys, are being cut open in an attempt to satisfy an apparently insatiable demand for sand and gravel currently running at over 100 million tons a year and likely to rise to over 600 million tons in south-east England alone by 1980, according to a 1974 report. Across in the South West, Cornwall has more derelict land than any other county in England, except West Yorkshire. Some 16,000 acres of this holiday county that many of us think of as all sunlit coves and old-world fishing villages is littered with grotesque white pyramids of china clay spoil heaps—admittedly admired by some poetic eyes—as well as with the detritus from tin mining. While the promised revival of tin mining hangs fire, the china-clay men are digging Britain's biggest hole on the fringe of the Dartmoor National Park at Lee Moor in neighbouring Devon. It will be $2\frac{1}{4}$ miles long, $1\frac{1}{2}$ miles wide and some 500ft deep in places, deep enough to take Salisbury Cathedral and its spire with 100ft to spare.

The Dartmoor Park is also threatened by a plan to carry out exploratory drilling for ball clay in the Bovey Basin, close to Bovey Tracey. The same company already mines clay near Wareham in Dorset and has mineral rights over 500 acres of Purbeck, but an application to extend workings on the Arne Peninsula was turned down in 1973.

In the late 1960s and early 1970s almost all Britain seemed in imminent danger of being ripped open in the search for minerals. Newspapers with conservationist consciences printed stories about three potash mines that were to be dug in the North Yorkshire Moors National Park, exploratory drilling for gold in the lovely Mawddach estuary, drilling for copper in the hills behind Dolgellau, for plutonium in north-west Scotland and for oil almost everywhere. Then Rio-Tinto Zinc, whose activities especially worried lovers of Wales, withdrew their planning application to search for gold in the Mawddach estuary, only one potash mine was sunk and press headlines became less terrifying as world prices of raw materials edged downwards. The danger, it seemed, was over for the moment. But that was

14

a mere breathing space. Now (1976) mineral prices are rising once more, the threat of those two additional potash mines hovers over the heather-clad moors of North Yorkshire, and a mining company hopes to be dredging tin-bearing sand just offshore in St Ives Bay by 1977. We must ask again if any area, however lovely, is sancrosanct.

At present the search for oil is mainly concentrated in the North Sea, and it is the landscape of Scotland that is most affected. But a Department of Energy report issued early in 1975 suggested that there could be at least 500 million tons of crude oil lying under 8,500 square miles of England and Wales. Within a month of that report's publication, licences were issued for exploratory drilling in the Midlands and elsewhere. If yields from the North Sea come up to expectations it may not be necessary to tap this reserve in the forseeable future, beyond the comparatively insignificant 100,000 tons or so that we get annually from the oil wells of Nottinghamshire, Lincolnshire and Kimmeridge Bay in Dorset without harming the environment. Anyone who wants to exploit these reserves further should be compelled to spend at least a year in West Lothian within sight of those mountainous 'bings', the spoil heaps that are ghastly memorials to the Scottish shale oil industry that survived from 1851 to 1963.

In many other areas also, new memorials are being erected to

2   Beauty and the beast: cement works in the Peak National Park

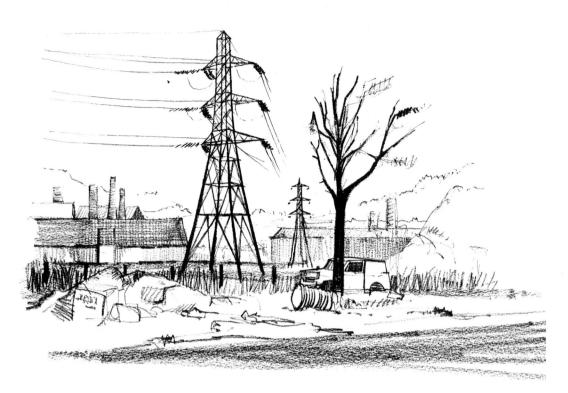

3 Such scenes of dereliction seem increasingly common

a vanishing Britain. Fresh heaps and holes disfigure the landscape of the East Midlands in the search for ironstone. Monstrous mechanical diggers tear out the clay of Bedfordshire beneath the shadows of enormous brick chimneys. Parts of the Downland of south-east England are pitted with ulcers of chalk, and hedges in once-rural parts of Nottinghamshire are white with dust from the gypsum that is being scraped out of neighbouring fields.

Other landscape wreckers

Mineral extractors, however, are not the only despoilers of the countryside. The Central Electricity Generating Board, the Post Office, even the broadcasting authorities have spoilt many good views with their towers and wires. From the window of a friend's hillside home in the Cotswolds I looked out recently across what had been a superb view until it was marred by two lines of overhead cable, one running right along the valley below, and the other, even more prominent, striding along the ridge above. There are places where pylons can add a touch of drama to a scene; but neither of these was such a place.

In fairness, though, it should be said that there have been occasions when the CEGB—and the Post Office too, for that matter—have co-operated in hiding power lines that would have marred and jarred. The use of the Woodhead Tunnel in the Peak Park to carry transmission lines underground for three miles was not only excellent engineering but a highly intelligent piece of conservation that prevented the ravelling of a wilderness in a wirescape. Several village scenes have been enhanced in

16

recent years by the removal of overhead wires. A particularly striking example is in the delightful National Trust village of Lacock in Wiltshire. Even the villagers' televisions operate—successfully, I am told—from a single communal aerial. Over the countryside as a whole, however, hang too many wires.

And they hang over a diminishing countryside. Although the pace of new road building may be slowing down for economic reasons, it will not stop in the foreseeable future, and a powerful motoring lobby would like more pressure on the accelerator. Most of us see the need for new roads—even new motorways—as long as they do not cut through our favourite beauty spots. But almost every mile of roadway spoils somebody's view, takes a slice of good farming land, involves the demolition of an attractive building and generally messes up the countryside.

Much has already been messed up by the armed forces, though there is no suggestion of their grabbing more land in the immediate future. On the contrary, they may surrender 22,500 acres, nearly a quarter of them in Dorset. This may sound quite generous until you reflect that it will still leave more than 600,000 acres in the hands of the Ministry of Defence, roughly the equivalent of the entire county of Staffordshire before reorganisation in April 1974.

If the land hunger of the Services has at least temporarily been assuaged, that of the towns has not. Although only about 11 per cent of Britain is built on—which seems surprisingly little—many of our towns are bulging disturbingly. 'Green belts' were an excellent idea, but unfortunately they are not sacrosanct. 'People have to live somewhere,' say councillors, begging a few important questions, and another slice of green belt gets a coating of red brick. From where I live, on the outer fringe of a provincial town, I could drive out into the country in three minutes, twenty years ago. Today it takes more than twice that time. Even beyond the green belts the villages are becoming suburban in quality, dormitories for commuters. And further out still, businessmen with cheque books at the ready await planning permission to build hypermarkets with massive car parks.

Redevelopment gone wrong

It is perhaps in the towns, especially the larger towns, however, that the old Britain is vanishing most rapidly. Some redevelopment was necessary in most towns, but the pace of urban change has been too violent for most townsfolk. Too much gold has been swept away with the dross. Redevelopment has become almost synonymous with destruction, and a reference to empty office blocks is invariably received with cynical smiles. The general effect has been to remove a great deal of individual character from the towns and reduce them to dull uniformity. It would be difficult now to feel, as James Boswell did in 1777, 'a pleasure . . . in walking about any town to which I am not

4 'Seventies Subtopia: this estate, on what was recently agricultural land, could be anywhere today

accustomed,' because it is becoming increasingly true that when you have been accustomed to one you have become accustomed to them all.

Boswell's remark was made about Derby, a town which exemplifies the point. Since the first edition of Pevsner's *Derbyshire* appeared in 1953—amongst the earlier of his *Buildings of England* series—the town has lost virtually three complete streets, two churches—with a third one likely to go—and more than a dozen other buildings of the limited number he thought worthy of mention. As Derby has for centuries tended to jettison its historic buildings, and had indeed before Pevsner's visit demolished its best half-timbered building to make way for an ugly gap that has never been filled, this case of rape aroused little more than a few mild grumbles in the town.

But while Derbeians fiddled, James Lees-Milne and others were burning, in the early 1960s, with justified rage at what became known as the 'Sack of Worcester'—the wanton destruction of ancient buildings in that city. There was even more widespread anger when the Euston Arch in 1961 was needlessly demolished against the advice of leading architects, in the station's rebuilding.

In a sense, the pointless demolition of the Euston Arch did more for conservation than any amount of angry writing could have done. It brought many people to their senses. The general public was at last roused by the enormity of the offence to say that this sort of official vandalism had to stop.

It has not in fact quite stopped. In 1975, Architectural Heritage Year, 350 buildings listed as of historic or architectural importance—Grade 2—were demolished. It is an appallingly high figure, but at least it is better than the 400 or so that were disappearing annually only a decade before, and no Grade I buildings vanished. And the net of listed buildings has been more widely spread; there were more than 230,000 at the end of 1975, compared with 118,000 in 1969. The proportion of destruction is down, but so, unfortunately, are too many good buildings that, like Humpty-Dumpty, can never be put together again.

What has changed, though, is the climate of opinion. It is no longer necessary to apologise for mentioning conservation or to defend it on purely economic grounds by speaking of the profits from tourism—while keeping quiet about the fact that tourism can be destructive by attracting too many bodies to too few places. If it is still too early to say that we are all conservationists now, it is true that many of us have become aware that we have lost much of our heritage and are in danger of losing more. A lot of good work has been done lately in preservation and restoration, while parliament has reflected this growing interest in the environment with some helpful protective legislation. But we are not yet winning the war against the despoilers of Britain. Too many places are still threatened by the kind of insensitive development that Lord Kennet fears; too many places that you should see now before it's too late.

2 Pressures on the Countryside

National Parks under siege

'A howling wilderness' was Daniel Defoe's dismissive description of the Derbyshire Peak at a time when Englishmen liked their scenery to be neat and serene. But in the 250 years or so since then, fashions in scenery, as in most other things, have changed. Nowadays, wildernesses are popular. Every year some 16 million people visit the Peak District National Park, a figure which has trebled in the last ten years. The nine other National Parks can all produce almost equally dramatic evidence of their growing attraction to tourists.

Not that the Peak is true wilderness, if you accept the purists' definition that a wilderness is an area more than ten miles from the nearest road, though it must have been in Defoe's day. But even today it has the appearance and atmosphere of a wilderness. You can be lost all too easily on the boggy plateaux of Kinder and Bleaklow, as indeed you can on parts of Dartmoor, the Lakeland fells, the North Yorkshire moors or the Brecon Beacons. It is because such areas have the stuff of wildness about them—a hint of menace, a touch of the elemental—that they have been chosen as national parks.

Only a minority of visitors stray into the wilder parts of the parks. Away from the more publicised paths, fell walkers in the Lake District can still find the sort of solitude that Wordsworth sought. You can walk all day on the North Yorkshire moors and not see more than three people. Most visitors are content to keep to the beaten tracks not too far from their motor cars, with the result that those tracks become not merely beaten but annihilated. The result of too many pairs of human feet treading on too small an area of the earth's surface is erosion of the topsoil and widespread destruction of plants.

This is what has happened at Tarn Hows and Dungeon Ghyll in the Lakes, Malham Tarn in the Yorkshire Dales, Dovedale in the Peak, Kinver Edge and parts of Cannock Chase, Staffordshire, some areas of the New Forest, Hampshire, Land's End, Cornwall, and many another over-popular beauty spot. There was a time when visitors came to these places only in summer, giving the vegetation a chance to recover during the long winter. But tourists' habits have changed during the last decade or so.

Prompted perhaps by a succession of mild winters and a little more money to spend on days out, people now tend to stretch their legs in the countryside throughout the year—good for human health, but not for vegetation.

This changing pattern of tourism and the near-permanent erosion problem that it causes has even affected parts of the Cairngorms, the dissected plateau that constitutes the largest area of genuine wilderness in Britain. The increasing popularity of winter sports has brought its special problems. Steel-edged skis damage plant life on hummocky ground, especially over peat. Bulldozers, increasingly used to make cheap dirt roads to ease the passage of sportsmen heading for the ski-slopes, break the vegetation cover, leaving the bare ground exposed. Surface water running downhill in the wake of the bulldozers soon washes out the soil and converts the new tracks into rock-strewn gullies. The washed-out sediment is squeezed outwards to bury vegetation on either side of the tracks. The short, slow-growing mountain plants, like the three-leaved rush and mountain wood-rush, in addition to the commoner bearberry, crowberry and heather, do not take kindly to burial. 2in of sediment can be enough to kill 95 per cent of mountain plant cover.

If these particular problems are peculiar to the Cairngorms, the area has not escaped the more general one of too many boots 'marching up and down again'. The constant tramping on the path between the ski-lift's top station and summit at Cairngorm has widened the track to 30yd in places. As the vegetation cover wore away, quantities of sediment washed off the path was deposited lower down the slope, burying more mountain plants. This path has been fenced off and walkers diverted to an alternative one, which is also deteriorating, but more slowly because it is less steep.

Similar remedial action has been taken in all the other places I have mentioned, but it has not always been easy, or cheap. The three-mile-long pathway through Dovedale, for instance, is extremely narrow in places and the steepness of the dale sides defy by-passing. Some remedial work has been done to help the path withstand the pressure of a half million pairs of feet a year, but the sort of thorough restoration scheme that the Peak Park authority had in mind would have cost £10,000 in 1972 and was just 'not on' at a time when public funds were being eroded just as quickly as the path through Dovedale, or, for that matter, on the summit of Snowdon, which is the subject of a financial wrangle.

The top of a mountain seems a most unlikely place to find erosion—unless, like the Grampians, it has a ski-run—or quarrels about money. But Snowdon, at 3,560ft the highest mountain south of the Scottish border, is a natural target for collectors of tallests and shortests as well as for those who want to see the incomparable view from the summit that, in my experience, was always at its finest yesterday before the clouds shut down and reduced visibility to a hundred yards. So every year some

210,000 optimists climb to the top, some tackling the difficult slopes, easing their way by tearing vegetation away from the rocks, a recognised climbing practice which is euphemistically called 'gardening' by climbers and harsher names by botanists. Others take the gentler paths and bridleways—not all that gentle near the top, as George Borrow found when he walked up from Llanberis in 1854. The remainder, almost half the total number of visitors, use the rack and pinion railway that takes about an hour to wheeze its way up from Llanberis.

Whichever method you choose, it is a rewarding experience, even if the clouds do cheat you of the view that the invariably fortunate Borrow saw: 'a scene inexpressibly grand, comprehending a considerable part of the mainland of Wales, the whole of Anglesey, a faint glimpse of part of Cumberland; the Irish Channel and what might be either a misty creation or the shadowy outline of the hills of Ireland'. What you are more likely to see on your way to the summit—apart from a 'misty creation'—are some of the mountain plants whose presence explains why most of Snowdon is a nature reserve. You may have to search very hard to find the holly fern, with its markedly spine-toothed fronds, woodsia fern and, especially, the Snowdon lily, all of which have been thinned out by over-enthusiastic collectors over the last three centuries, but there are still quantities of pink moss campion, purple saxifrage, vernal sandwort, rose-root—a succulent plant which derives its name from the smell of its stout rootstock—Alpine meadow-rue, Alpine scurvy-grass, whose leaves and stems have such high vitamin-C content, mountain sorrel and the rock-loving mossy saxifrage.

Unfortunately, none of these is likely to be found on the summit itself or very close to the tracks. Baldness is creeping up on the mountain top as inexorably as it does on the head of an ageing man, which is hardly surprising when you reflect that about 2,500 people wander around the summit on a fine day in July and August.

The damage is not irreparable, but restoration will be costly. Who is going to pay for it? This question, not for the first time, led to the row. From the deliberations of the bodies most concerned with Snowdon—the Countryside Commission, Gwynedd County Council and the Snowdonia National Park Committee—there emerged a strong feeling that those who, as somebody said, were 'making a molehill out of a mountain' should pay. That means the public, you and me. But how to make people pay for using a mountain? Toll gates and uniformed attendants are obvious non-starters. Whether the public should be made to pay for the enjoyment of the countryside and fresh air, two of the few free pleasures left to us, is a still more important question that needs much thought before a final answer is given, although the Ramblers' Association have already come up with their answer: in essence it is much the same as that given by Shaw's Eliza Doolittle to Freddy Eynsford-Hill in *Pygmalion*!

Most of us would probably give the same answer, but from the lips of a motorist it might have a slightly hollow sound, for there is some justice in the suggestion that the motorist might pay a little more—perhaps in increased parking fees—for the damage he causes. If the motorist replies, with some heat, that you cannot get a car anywhere near the summit of Snowdon and he is therefore blameless, I must counter by saying that it is nearly always a car that gets him to the foot of the mountain. The pressures on Snowdon, and most other near-wilderness areas, are largely the product of the motor age.

5 Human erosion: damage caused by countless feet on Kinver Edge, Staffordshire, can be seen in the foreground; the firmer path has been put down as part of a rescue operation

Motorway madness

More than ten thousand cars enter the Lake District National Park on a single fine summer Sunday. Nevertheless, a National Trust report in the summer of 1974 claimed that there was no major traffic problem within the park. The traffic queues that made press headlines were usually on the approach roads on the fringes of the area. Admittedly, that was just before the opening of the Kendal by-pass which brought fast traffic to within seven miles of the eastern shores of Lake Windermere and put the Lake District within day-trip range of 20 million people, but it is still possible, as in most other national parks, to motor in fair comfort off the main roads, if only because the average motorist seems unwilling or unable to read a map. Walking—off the

23

valley roads, of course—is more comfortable still. Indeed it has been suggested that the fells are more empty now than they were 60 years ago when the motor car was still a rarity. More visitors now seem unwilling to move away from their homes on wheels, whether these be just single cars or the caravans that on Bank Holiday weekends clog every lay-by between Keswick and Kendal.

Most national park authorities agree that one of their biggest problems is temporarily blocked arteries, the clogging up of a few main roads in a few places for a few hours on a few days of the year. Various forms of treatment have been prescribed in different areas, all designed to disperse the blockages. The Northumberland, Pembrokeshire and Peak District National Parks all encourage people to leave their cars at home, or park them on the fringes of popular areas, and use midi- or mini-bus services, linked with service buses from farther afield, within congested areas. The Peak board, with Countryside Commission support, pioneered a scheme—since followed elsewhere—of closing the narrow Goyt Valley lanes at busy times to all but access traffic and their own mini-buses. So far, these policies, and various experiments with 'scenic routes' for tourists, have eased the severity of the disease, and so, to a lesser degree, have various schemes for hiring out bicycles to explore popular areas. Given time, these dispersal projects, coupled with the present reduction in motoring, may save our wilder beauty spots from vanishing behind long queues of stationary vehicles.

New and vastly 'improved' roads are certainly no remedy. They not only tear up lovely landscapes but bring in their wake more motor cars at higher speeds to cause more congestion which has to be eased by further new and 'improved' roads. On top of that—or at the side—comes all the paraphernalia of filling stations, cafés and forests of concrete lamp standards, like those that have brought a taste of central Manchester into the Lake District at the Stainton roundabout, where that heavenly scenic road from Newby Bridge and Ullswater comes down to earth with a jolt as it meets the A66.

'Is there no nook of English ground secure from rash assault?' Wordsworth once demanded on hearing of some potential desecration of his beloved Lakeland. If that piece of insensitivity at Stainton might have provoked some similiar response, the proposal to widen that same A66 to dual carriageways for two miles along the eastern shore of Lake Bassenthwaite could have achieved the almost impossible by leaving even him speechless with horror. As it was, other voices, those of the Friends of the Lake District and the Council for the Protection of Rural England among the loudest, were raised in protest against a piece of official vandalism that will bring more heavy lorry traffic through the Lake District and clip a modest seven minutes off the time it should take the motorist from Penrith to drive to Cockermouth, compared with a less devastating suggested alternative. Why, asked the voices, a dual carriageway in that

particularly beautiful spot when most of the rest of the rou.
is single carriageway? That question has not been answered
satisfactorily and it looks as if climbers on Skiddaw will soon have
to look down on a lakeside shorn of its fringe of trees, and
sprouting instead a 24ft macadam ribbon and a concrete embank-
ment bulging out 'into the margin of the lake'.

Even this enormity palls beside the threat of a motorway
that would decapitate the Peak National Park to provide a direct
route between Manchester and Sheffield. It would cut through
the neck of the Park along the Longdendale Valley, 'a treeless
moorland of immense proportions and far horizons', an empty
wilderness much treasured by lovers of solitude and hard walking
(illustration 6).

Not quite empty, says the motorway lobby, as the valley is
already disfigured by reservoirs, an overhead power line, an
electrified railway line and the A628(T) road. This argument
seems unshakable until you go to see for yourself. It looks then
less substantial. Railway, power line and road are there all right,
but nestling in the valley bottom. They do not stride across the
mat-grass of the flanking hillsides as would the proposed M67.
The power line is a bit of an eyesore, but, like the railway, it
tunnels for three miles under the high moorland between Woodhead and Dunford Bridge. Only the A628 crosses the Woodhead
Pass and intrudes on the moors where meadow pipits nest and

6 Longdendale Pass, Derbyshire
threatened by the proposed M67
between Sheffield and Manchester

7 Havoc caused by major road improvements at Cadnam in the New Forest

curlews cry overhead. Little more than 22ft wide, it fits quite snugly into the topography. A six-lane motorway rising 550ft on to the Pennines in five miles between Torside and Carr Top would force the roadmakers to treat natural features as obstacles, as on the M62 which crosses the Pennines on a parallel line only 11 miles further north. It would cut through hills as the M62 does at Windy Hill and the M1 through Charnwood Forest, be supported by embankments on steeply sloping valley sides and stride across gorges and cloughs on massive viaducts as at Rakewood on the M62.

Such a project would be costly in terms of money and lost amenities. It would be the first motorway to cut through a national park. Is it really worth creating such a dangerous precedent for a scheme that, desirable as it may look from the boardrooms of Sheffield and Manchester, hardly seems essential?

A rather similar question has already been asked by lovers of Epping Forest, which appears destined to have a quarter of a mile nibbled off its outer crust by a six-lane motorway, the M16, that will link Waltham Cross with Brentwood. The question may have been phrased differently, as the Forest is neither a national park nor a wilderness, but it is in distance and atmosphere the nearest approximation that Londoners have to either. So the question here was whether it is ever necessary to slice a chunk of roadway out of a well defined, much loved area that, in this case, has already lost its red and roe deer and many of its fallow deer and badgers because of increasing traffic pressures.

26

The answer was, in effect, that economic needs must come first. The only concessions road-builders were prepared to offer to conservation—and to the powerful Corporation of London, who are guardians of the Forest—were two special animal subways and an overhead route to allow the remaining fallow deer to reach their hinterlands outside the Forest, in addition to stretches of 'cut and cover', trenched road artificially roofed.

Must economic needs always come first, though? Is the planner to regard all other considerations as luxuries, like Shaw's Andrew Undershaft? In times like the present, you feel inclined to say 'yes', however reluctantly, but then go to areas like Dartmoor, the Peak, the Mendips or eastern Shropshire, and you are forced to think again.

Mines and quarries

That Dartmoor should be facing industrial pressures may come as a surprise to people outside the South West who think of the Moor as the preserve of ponies, Uncle Tom Cobley and the Hound of the Baskervilles, and remember that H. V. Morton once called it 'the green Sahara of England'. But mineral extractors have been hacking away at that desert for at least eight centuries and perhaps much more, taking tin, copper, iron, lead, arsenic and even some of its granite, leaving behind lunar-like craters, including one that supplied the stone for Nelson's Column in Trafalgar Square.

Today, though, granite is extracted from only one quarry, and china clay production is Dartmoor's only major industry. It is confined to the Moor's south-west corner, a curiously Cornish-looking area where many self-exiled Cornishmen are engaged in excavating away the skyline to help produce bone china, news-papers and other products that make important contributions to Britain's export trade. The 500 inhabitants of Lee Moor, many of Cornish descent, like to boast that their village, which sprang up in the nineteenth century to serve the industry, exports more goods than any other village of its size in England. If permission is received for an extension to china clay workings there, those exports will increase—and Dartmoor's beauty diminish.

The same sort of decision between the merits of beauty and the economic beast will be made soon about an extension to limestone quarrying in Great Rocks Dale in the limestone up-lands of the Derbyshire Peak. Great Rocks Dale is a deep, winding, dry dale, opening at its southern end into that lovely Wye Gorge that is successively called Wye Dale, Chee Dale, Miller's Dale and Monsal Dale as the river winds towards its confluence with the Derwent. There must have been a time, I suppose, when Great Rocks Dale rivalled these neighbours for beauty. But in the 1860s the railwaymen came and drove through it their main Midland line between St Pancras and Manchester, and in their wake came the quarrymen to pick and hack at those great rocks that gave the valley its name. Between them they turned a lovely valley into an inferno of smoking lime-kilns, huge blasted misshapen craters and a film of grey limestone dust as if every ash-tray in Britain had been simultaneously emptied across the face of the land. Because of this, the planners drawing up the boundaries of the Peak Park—the first of our national parks—apparently took a pair of scissors, snipped a narrow salient out of Peak District, closed the Park gates against it and left it to wallow in its own dust.

Unfortunately the quarrymen were not content to remain permanently outside the pale. In 1973, ICI, owners of Tunstead Quarry in Great Rocks Dale, already the largest quarry in Europe, sought planning permission to extend the workings for 200yd inside the Park at Wormhill. The Peak Park Board, the planning authority, turned down the application because the existing workings contained enough limestone to last out this century. But as I write, a public enquiry at Buxton is hearing a renewed application, and the villagers of Wormhill await its outcome anxiously, wondering if they will be sitting on the edge of a vast crater in the year 2000.

By that time the face of the Mendips will have drastically changed. If quarrying continues, predicts W. I. Stanton, author of *Man and the Mendips*, 'half of Sandford Hill, one fifth of Callow Hill, and huge chunks of Mendip east of Shipham Gorge and north of Cheddar will have gone,' assuming a projected annual rate of 20 million tons.

You can see the shape of things to come if you approach Cheddar from the direction of Wells or Wedmore. Cheddar Gorge may be, as a recent writer has said, 'the most commercialised natural phenomenon in the West Country,' but it still has beauty that deserves a better introduction than the machinery and spoil-heaps of Callow Rock Quarry rising above the skyline at 800ft to greet the visitor coming up from the south. Cheddar village itself, famous for caves, cheese and coach parties, is dominated by the multiple face—more than 500yd wide and 400ft high—of Batts Combe quarry, the biggest in the West Mendips.

To condemn the Mendips as an abomination of desolation on the strength of quarrying round Cheddar would be foolish. Despite its blemishes, this is still an attractive if slightly austere area of grassy rounded hills, stone walls and stone-built villages nestling mainly in south-facing combes sheltered from the searching winds that blow across the tops. It is a tract of land remarkably like the central uplands of the Derbyshire Peak, with a similar history of mineral exploitation from Roman lead miners to the twentieth-century quarry owners tearing out its heart to get at the limestone that accounts for the family resemblance to Derbyshire.

Now both areas face similar dangers, but the greater threat is to Mendip which lacks the protection of national-park status. East Mendip seems likely to fare as badly as the west. By the year 2000, 'the hills north-east of Gurney Slade will have been

flattened, . . . about one quarter of the limestone outcrop between Stoke St Michael and Leigh on Mendip will have vanished . . . little limestone will be left in the region between Chantry, Mells, Great Elm and Whatley. Of the large area of limestone enclosed by the villages of Downhead, Nunney, Leighton, Granmore and Heale, more than one third will have been removed.' This is not alarmist speculation, says Dr Stanton, 'The planning consent already exists.'

In too many areas, planning permission was rashly doled out for quarrying and mineral extraction in the 1940s and early 1950s when conservation was still considered synonymous with crankishness. Once given, such consent cannot be revoked without the offer of another site of equal value or the payment of compensation based on future earnings, as Shropshire people have discovered to their chagrin.

In this hitherto relatively unspoilt county where the late P. G. Wodehouse, with his unerring sense of place, located his perpetually sun-drenched Blandings Castle, there are only about ten quarries, several operating under planning permission granted in the late 1940s. One of these, unfortunately, has already done much damage to Wenlock Edge, that splendid limestone ridge that runs for twenty miles from Much Wenlock to Craven Arms.

8 How many previously unspoilt areas are now disfigured by similar sights?

It has been said to look 'like a great wave about to break' over a delicious green countryside that inspired the once widely acclaimed prose of the now half-forgotten Mary Webb and much of the poetry of A. E. Housman. When Housman wrote 'On Wenlock Edge the wood's in trouble' he was thinking of the effects of a gale rather than of two landslips that brought many magnificent beech trees sliding 40ft into the quarry below and left others overhanging the quarry edge awaiting another slip. Ironically, the 'wood's in trouble' on the opposite side of the Edge too, because a private landowner is clearing the remaining 120 acres of an ancient deciduous woodland at the rate of about 10 acres a year and replacing the hardwood mainly with quicker-growing conifers. This may be good management, but it seems a pity that Wenlock Edge should be losing trees on both sides concurrently.

The quarrying inflicts the more damage, however, as it does a few miles further east around the Wrekin, that astonishing pyramid of a hill that rises abruptly out of the Midland Plain to a summit at 1,355ft. The Wrekin is not, by quite a long way, Shropshire's highest hill, but it is the one that inspires the greatest affection in the hearts of most Salopians, mainly, I suppose, because it is visible over much of the county and far beyond. I have seen it from Axe Edge, with the whole width of Staffordshire in between, and I can understand why a returning 'Shropshire Lad' presses a little harder on his accelerator pedal on catching a first glimpse of that lofty cone. For him it symbolises home, and the thought that anyone might be despoiling that home must certainly cause a sharp rise in blood pressure.

So far, nobody has laid hands on the Wrekin itself, but great bites have been taken out of its foothills, Lawrence's Hill, the apple-shaped Maddock's Hill and that miniature replica of the Wrekin called Ercall Hill. Woodlands round their bases have been torn away to permit the passage of quarrying machines. Maddock's Hill looks like a half-cracked, half-eaten boiled egg, so that even some ardent conservationists accept that its top might as well be levelled off and removed for roadstone rather than left in its miserably maimed state. Certainly nobody wants it or its consorts left in the same devastated state as those abandoned slate quarries over the Welsh border around Blaenau Ffestiniog and Llanberis.

Ordeal by water

Seen on a wet day there is nothing more depressing than those mutilated mountains of black Welsh slate. But in the sunshine, as I saw them last on a late August afternoon in the glorious summer of 1975, those vast worked-out terraces of Dinorwic Quarry on the slopes of Elidir above the Llanberis Pass take on a pleasing shade of purple which I had not noticed before. That afternoon I saw something else that surprised me: rubble being cleared from the terraces and tipped into worked-out pits by tipper lorries that scurried out of hillside holes like rabbits from a burrow. I was glad, I remarked to a passer-by, to see that an eyesore was being removed. 'Yes,' he said, 'to make way for a bigger eyesore.'

He could be right. What those tiny ant-like figures and their toy-sized lorries were doing up there, high on the slopes of Elidir, was making space to build Europe's largest pumped storage plant, a close relative of the more conventional hydro-electric system, and a more distant, vastly larger relative of the domestic storage heater.

The power, sufficient to provide all Wales with peak-hour electricity, will be obtained by allowing water from Marchlyn Mawr, a lake 2,000ft above sea level on the summit of Elidir, to pour through a two-mile tunnel in the mountain. On its way the torrent of water will power six turbine generators in Europe's largest underground power station before cascading into Llyn Peris, the smaller of the two Llanberis lakes. During a six-hour off-peak period, the water will be pumped back uphill from Peris to Marchlyn.

All this will involve the building of a giant dam at Marchlyn and two smaller ones at Peris, ten miles of new and improved roads, and constant changes in the water levels of both lakes to the discomfiture of the char, those hill trout that still inhabit the cold depths of Peris as they did in Defoe's time. Llyn Peris, lying right alongside one of Britain's busiest touring routes, is one of Snowdonia's best known lakes. Those who have not seen it, and want to while it is undisturbed, should do so before 1981 when the Dinorwic Pumped Storage Scheme is due for completion—or preferably earlier still before the mess becomes too noticeable.

Long before 1981 a new, artificial lake will have been con-structed in the valley of the North Tyne, new homes will have been found for the inhabitants of the hamlet of Plashetts, and the appearance of this particular stretch of wilderness in northern England will have changed for the second time in half a century. In 1926 this area stretching from Carter Bar on the Scottish border southward into the hinterland of Northumberland was a rather desolate, almost treeless, humpy landscape of fine bent grass. That was the year the Forestry Commission started planting spruce, larch and pine in what is now the 200 square mile Border Forest Park, the largest forest area in Britain. A portion of this, just above the village of Falstone, is now to disappear under a new Kielder Reservoir. Soon the Kielder Youth Hostel, forest land, grazing land and Plashetts will all have disappeared under 70ft of water. The landscape will be transformed; it may to some eyes be improved. A large stretch of water imposed on this sort of wide, open landscape can look most effective—if one can ignore an obviously man-made dam.

Many people do like reservoirs, even those from which sailing and other aquatic activities are barred. Britons love gazing at open stretches of water, and as an ex-sailor, I must admit to a certain nostalgic indulgence in this occupation. But a reservoir

9 A typical Dartmoor clapper bridge which has so far managed to survive the annual tourist onslaught, unlike many of the Moor's tors which are gradually wearing away

looks too urban, its landscaping too carefully contrived, like the new Meldon reservoir which now covers the once lovely West Okement Valley on Dartmoor. In the apt words of Eric Newby, it 'bears an uncanny resemblance to a flooded municipal convenience'.

Dartmoor, like the Peak, is under constant threat of ordeal by water. Local preservationists may win a long battle to prevent the construction of another reservoir at Swincombe, south of Princetown, but if they do they may have to fight elsewhere, with Bickleigh, Roadford or Townleigh as possible venues.

Small-scale beauty in danger

If areas of outstanding beauty, like Dartmoor and other places internationally known, many with national park status and powerful local preservationist groups, are under constant pressure from builders of reservoirs, roads, power stations, quarries, or even from too many people and too many motor cars, what hope is there for the preservation of places that lie off the usual tourist map? I am thinking of those pleasant places that do not draw immediate gasps of admiration and wonderment, are not spoken of in awed capitals as 'our British Heritage', but are enjoyed by local people and sometimes by a few from further afield who have discovered them perhaps by chance.

Otmoor is a good example. If it is split by an extension of the M40 or drowned under a new reservoir to slake London's thirst—and both are real possibilities—people outside Oxfordshire are unlikely to be deeply stirred, for though only some seven miles north-east of Oxford it is a surprisingly remote area that guide-book writers have called 'the forgotten land' and, in more lyrical passages, 'bewitched Otmoor'.

It is a stretch of wild fenland, covering some 4,000 acres, that seems closer in spirit to East Anglia than the south-west Midlands. Commuters have not invaded 'sleeping Otmoor' because no civil engineer has attempted to cut a road across it since the Romans, with imperious disdain for flood hazards, constructed their route from Dorchester to Alchester, near Bicester. This today is just one of a number of boggy green tracks crossing an area that is a riot of wild roses and blackthorn in spring and a paradise for wild-fowl and rare wild flowers. Engineers planning a road across Otmoor will have to consider not only the marshy terrain but also the equally intractable attitude of the natives, bearing in mind the violent riots that followed the eighteenth-century Enclosure Acts. Force was used then to uphold the law, and the landscape took on that chequered appearance that later suggested to Lewis Carroll, viewing the moor from the rim of encircling higher ground, the idea of the human chess game in *Alice in Wonderland*. Blows might not be exchanged in the 1970s, but the speed with which a powerful Otmoor Defence committee was formed at the first hint of a prospective reservoir suggests that the mood of the natives has changed as little as their delightful villages. The reservoir threat may have receded a little and the course of the road has yet to be settled, but in places like Beckley, Oddington and Charlton-on-Otmoor the inhabitants are ready to resist any attempt to change Otmoor's character.

Thorne Moor (or Waste) is a vaguely similar if less beautiful stretch of fenland, just north-east of Doncaster in Yorkshire, that seems destined to die a more lingering, less spectacular death from peat extraction and, possibly, the dumping of power station ash, lamented only by naturalists and a few people with tastes for strange, deserted, atmospheric places. A fondness for Thorne Moor may be an acquired, esoteric taste, but for those who have picked it up there is no putting it down. In medieval times it was oak and pine forest, but after clearance it deteriorated into a vast morass supporting many rare plants. Today, after more than a century of peat extraction, burning and increased drainage from a network of channels, it has shrunk to just over 4,000 acres—roughly the same as Otmoor—and its character is changing. Much of it is a cold, desolate wilderness of bracken, heather, cotton grass, reeds and rushes, invaded in places by birch and willow. Some of the less acid land now lies under the plough, which has destroyed the habitat of milk parsley, marsh pea and pen violet, but the rare bog rosemary has survived and the fen sedge and royal fern that were thought to be extinct have re-established themselves. It is still the haunt of such protected birds as the hobby falcon, the kingfisher, the barn owl and the little ringed plover. It is also the only known British home of a bright bronze-coloured beetle, *Bemidion humerale*. Even so, the moor it not what it was, but it is worth going to see, once anyway, while it retains some individuality. Unless you are a keen naturalist, you may hate it, but there is chance that you may be drawn back time after time.

Much the same may be said of Hatfield Chase, a former royal

10 The wild, wet wasteland of Rannoch Moor, Perthshire retains its bleak beauty

forest, lying immediately south of Thorne Moor, as it may of the neighbouring, larger, more cultivated and populous Isle of Axeholme, and as it certainly may of Sedgemoor in Somerset. Sedgemoor's spell is perhaps the most pervasive of them all, if only because it is hard to resist places with names like Weston Zoyland and Chedzoy rolling off the lips of Somerset country-men and with church towers that are impressive even by Somerset standards. In less than half a century all the peat will have been scooped out of Sedgemoor. The portion called Shapwick Heath will have become a large hole extending over an area of four square miles. That is how the Norfolk Broads were formed. Will Shapwick Heath become another broad and a tourist attraction? Or will it become another reservoir? For better or worse, the appearance of Shapwick Heath will have changed.

So will that of two areas of Derbyshire near my home, one threatened by a motorway, the other by a reservoir. Because I know them well and cherish them dearly, they symbolise for me exactly the type of landscape I have been talking about: far too attractive to spoil but not sufficiently dramatic to be able to save when 'realists' with their heads firmly dug in the sand say 'but we must have roads' or, 'but where is our water to come from?'

One is just a belt of quiet grassland in south-west Derbyshire, occupied more by cattle and sheep than by the people in remote farmhouses and scattered villages with names like Marston Montgomery, Long Lane and Great Cubley, great only in comparison with Little Cubley, linked by inconsequential lanes that twist and wander with no regard for the convenience of the thrusting motorist. There are no guide-book 'beauty spots' and consequently no tourists. It is the sort of country that Constable

34

might have painted; timeless, relaxing, very English—the very qualities that do not lend themselves to exact definition at a public inquiry, but qualities that will be missed if a Stoke-on-Trent–Derby motorway strides across this small-scale landscape.

The other area I have in mind lies ten miles or so north-eastward. There, among the Peak foothills and therefore overlooked by tourists heading for the more spectacular country in the National Park, the Scow Brook may be damned and the valley flooded. The nearest villages—Carsington, Hopton and Hognaston—will not be directly affected. That is, their grey stone houses will remain intact, though there will have to be a new road to by-pass Carsington and Hopton, and another for Hognaston, running along a dam for three quarters of a mile, and just one or two outlying farms will have to go. The farmers affected are not among those who say the reservoir 'will be good for trade and bring new life to the area', which is a fairly common reaction in the few pubs and shops thereabouts when thoughts turn to the picnickers, anglers and water-sports enthusiasts who might make a playground of a new reservoir.

There is, I suppose, nothing special about this valley of the Scow Brook; just lush, rolling fields still separated by hedgerows teeming with wildlife, a variety of trees including still-healthy wych elms planted by the Gell family who have lived at Hopton since medieval times, an ambling lane or two and a few green tracks, and on the encircling slopes belts of thicker woodlands with names like Lendow Wood, Old Wood, Big Covert, Hall Wood, Carr Wood and Pen Carr. It all amounts to nothing very dramatic, but its serene beauty would be missed greatly by many people besides myself if it vanished underwater.

3 The Threat to Wildlife

Chemical pollution

The changes that have been taking place in the countryside have obviously affected its wildlife. It would be difficult now to wade 'through a sea of tall brown-knotted rushes to watch the glorious peacocks and tortoiseshells imbibing sweetness from the favourite blossoms' as did Norfolk naturalist E. A. Ellis on a shimmering hot August afternoon in Broadland just after World War II. The 'old-rose tassels of hemp agrimony, delicate pink spires of marsh woundwort, magenta-purple loosestrife, button-heads of knap-weed and nectarous marsh thistles' are much harder to find now around these 1,700 acres of open water and about 90 miles of navigable channels that make up that increasingly popular holiday area, the Norfolk Broads.

Something very unpleasant happened to the Broads in the early 1970s, as scientists from the University of East Anglia discovered when they surveyed 28 of the 40 or so broads. They found 11 to be completely devoid of aquatic vegetation and another 11 only supporting very feeble plant growth. In several only water-lilies grew. As the plants provide the organisms on which fish feed, the fish stocks are consequently declining. What until a few years ago were among the country's best coarse fisheries now offer little sport for the angler and little food for such bottom-feeding birds as coots and swans, whose numbers show a similar decline. The booming of the bittern among the reeds, a common sound less than a decade ago, is rarely heard now, and the marsh harrier has gone altogether. 'The richest and most varied freshwater habitat in Britain' that Robert Arvill described in *Man and the Environment* as recently as 1967 is now in danger of becoming 'a fen of stagnant water'.

Nobody is yet sure what has caused this rapid decline. The Broads have always kept their secrets well. Not until the 1950s was it established beyond reasonable doubt that they were formed not as had been thought by geological accident but by medieval man digging for peat. Over the centuries a gradual, natural silting up has caused some worries, and this century has added two new problems. One has been lack of management, following the decline of traditional crafts like thatching and the cultivation of forage for horses, which has hastened the silting

36

process and encouraged an overgrowth of vegetation. The second has been increasing human pressure on a comparatively small area. Broadland has beckoned urgently to the holidaymaker seeking the peace of quiet waterways and teeming wildlife and, in answering the invitation, he has inevitably helped to destroy both.

As the century advanced, the sailing dinghy gave way to the motor-boat which caused increasing pollution and erosion of banks. In 1967 there were about 5,500 launches and cruisers and some 2,500 sailing vessels on the Broads. By 1973 there were nearly 14,000 boats of all kinds. The end of the century may see 20,000 vessels on these waterways, more than half of them motor-driven.

Some people put all the blame for the decline of Broadland's wildlife on boat-users. Turbidity caused by boats stirring up mud from the bottom could certainly be a factor. So could pollution from rubbish tipped over boats' sides, though all holiday craft now have to be equipped with chemical toilets and only washing-up water can legally go untreated into the Broads and rivers. But though boat-users cannot be exonerated from blame for the Broadland disaster, the chief suspects seem to be the industrialist and the farmer.

An increase of sewage effluent pouring into the main rivers, it is argued, could be the main cause of the trouble, a theory supported by the fact that broads linked to the main river systems have suffered more than the smaller isolated ones. Another school of thought puts the blame on excessive use of agricultural fertiliser either in the production of sugar beet or in turning the old grazing marshes into arable fields. This change in land use involves heavy dressings of fertiliser containing

11 Outwardly unspoiled, Lyme Regis, Dorset, is one of 95 seaside towns that still pump untreated sewage into the sea

37

phosphates and nitrogen which, it is suggested, are washed into the broads to create a death trap for wildlife, especially for fish, so susceptible to quite low quantities of poison.

What ever its main cause, the 'death of the Broads', as the disaster was perhaps over-dramatically described in 1975, was only one particularly horrifying incident in a series of accidents that have struck at British wildlife in the last twenty years or so. Nearly everyone will remember the myxomatosis plague, 'the most momentous event in the English countryside since the Black Death', that was somehow carried—deliberately, some say—from France to Edenbridge in Kent in the late summer of 1953 and raged over most of Britain for the next two years, wiping out almost the entire rabbit population from some areas. Memories being short, fewer people may recall that the death-rate among birds in some parts of Britain was almost as heavy in the late 1950s and early 1960s as it had been among the rabbit population, though the cause was different.

The sharp rise in bird mortality followed the first use by farmers, in about 1956, of organochlorine seed dressings, such as aldrin, dieldrin, heptchlor or DDT, to combat wireworm and wheat bulb fly. Wood pigeons and rooks suffered worst, but pheasants, partridges and greenfinches were found dead in ever-increasing numbers. In the spring of 1961 nearly 6,000 birds were found dead at Tumby in Lincolnshire. Birds of prey, seemingly unaffected at first by the poison, eventually suffered cruelly. The sparrowhawk, having survived its long war with gamekeepers, nearly vanished from Britain, buzzards dwindled in number, as did kestrels from the high farming areas of eastern England, and the peregrine falcon population was almost literally decimated. Apart from the buzzards, which may have been poisoned by insecticides used in sheep dip and passed on through carrion, the evidence suggests that most predators died through secondary poisoning. To put it another way, the predator might feed on a smaller bird, such as a thrush, which had already consumed a poisoned earthworm. Thus the poison entered the food chain and doses would gradually be released into the bloodstream, causing death in times of food shortage, reproduction or migration.

The killing had to stop. After the first holocaust, some semblance of peace returned to the countryside thanks to the investigations carried out by such voluntary bodies as the Royal Society for the Protection of Birds and the British Trust for Ornithology, followed by pressure at the highest levels by the Nature Conservancy Board. In 1962 a voluntary armistice was declared on the use of organochlorine seed dressings on spring-sown grain, and the mortality rate among small birds sharply declined. A census taken by the British Trust for Ornithology in 42 areas of farmland in 1963 showed a rise of 8 per cent in the chaffinch population over the previous year. Birds of prey took longer to recover, but the sparrowhawks now seem to be flourishing and you seldom drive along a motorway without seeing a kestrel hovering overhead ready to pounce on some victim on that unofficial nature reserve, the central reservation.

More than a decade later, the truce on spring dressing is still loyally observed by most farmers and pesticide companies, but many conservationists would like to see it made compulsory as recommended by the Cook Commission in 1967. As things stand, autumn-sown dressed grain can pass on dieldrin to kill both field mice and the barn owls, tawny owls and kestrels that feed on them. Accidents still sometimes happen. In the winter of 1974–5 hundreds of greylag geese, a winter migrant from the Arctic, died in Britain, apparently as a result of eating a seed dressing containing the chemical carbophenothion that had been approved by the Ministry of Agriculture for controlling bulb fly in wheat crops. The strange thing about this pesticide is that it is known to have been eaten in large quantities by other species of birds without apparent ill-effects.

Despite such accidents, we must accept that pesticides and herbicides are necessary for modern economic farming and here to stay. With their help, the yield per acre for most home-produced crops was higher in 1974 than ever before. More than 52 per cent of the food on our table comes from British farms, compared with less than 48 per cent twenty years ago. This sort of result from agricultural land that is dwindling at the rate of about 55,000 acres annually 'can't be bad'—to use a vogue phrase—for either housewife or farmer. But as with medicinal drugs on humans, these chemical agricultural 'drugs' can produce harmful side-effects if they are not carefully handled. For example, the red spider mite that was a nuisance to fruit farmers was often kept in check by its natural enemies, but so many of these have been destroyed by pesticides that the mites have emerged as more serious pests than before.

Disappearing hedgerows

As with chemical fertilisers and the like, so with hedges—or without them. To grub up a few internal hedges that form no property boundary but merely divide fields arbitrarily seems sensible enough in these days of highly mechanised farming. But a drastic clearance is liable to be followed by the sort of dust storm that swept across the Lincoln–Grantham road a few years ago, carrying with it the light topsoil of some unfortunate farmer who had incautiously erased a hedge too many.

'Without hedges, England would not be England,' wrote Richard Jeffries when he saw hedges grubbed up to make way for the steam plough nearly a century ago. But in that false dawn of mechanised farming, Jeffries had perhaps forgotten that England had once been a land, if not quite without hedges, certainly with less than half the number that criss-cross our countryside today.

A slice of that pre-enclosure England survives at Laxton, just south of Tuxford in a thinly populated rural area of Nottingham-shire. The village retains its medieval layout with the red pantile-roofed farms strung out along the two streets on narrow strips of land. The farm buildings are adjacent, the kitchen gardens, orchards and crofts behind. Just beyond the houses are the three big open fields of about 300 acres each, still worked in strips in the medieval fashion. It is an astonishing survival of an older England, and it is not likely to vanish now that the Ministry of Agriculture has become lord of the manor of Laxton and intends to preserve the open-field system as a sort of living museum.

Laxton is an attractive village. The open landscape around is fresh, invigorating—but somehow incomplete. You may have to make two or three visits before you realise—what the trained naturalist will notice immediately—that what are missing are the ordinary farm birds. There are skylarks, lapwing, a few grey partridge and red-legged partridge; a careful survey revealed one pair of reed bunting in a hollow. Apart from this solitary pair of marsh or stream birds, all are birds of the open field. Many of the common birds that breed in hedgerows can be found in enclosed land outside the village, but not in the open fields. Mammals are more elusive anyway, and so far as I know there has been no survey of Laxton's mammals, but many are creatures of the hedgerow—the hedgehog, surprisingly, less so than most—and I suspect that they are equally scarce in Laxton.

This is one reason why those country-lovers who would welcome a return to an open pre-enclosure landscape are outnumbered by those who regret the loss of probably more than one fifth of Britain's estimated 500,000 miles of hedgerow in the last twenty years or so. Another reason is the effect of this loss on the appearance of the countryside. Vast hedgeless fields may be acceptable in the clear wide-skied landscape of East Anglia and the south-east Midlands, but the more intimate landscape of central and south-western England demands its chequerboard pattern of small fields divided by those hedgerow trees that provide shelter for animals, protection from wind and immense delight to country-lovers. A third reason is historical, for not all hedges date from the enclosure movements. Some have stood marking boundaries since Saxon times. Using the theory advanced by Dr Max Hooper of the Nature Conservancy's Monk Wood research station in Huntingdonshire that hedges support one shrub species for every 100 years of age or thereabouts, W. G. Hoskins estimated that the southern hedge-bank of Church Farm at Cadbury in mid-Devon was constructed about 900, possibly in the lifetime of Alfred the Great. If Hooper is right, the destruction of hedges not only disfigures the countryside but removes roughly datable historical artifacts—important tools of the historian's trade.

Yet that destruction continues. We are still losing each year, according to a 1975 CPRE estimate, a little over 4,000 miles of those 'hedges, thick and high and full of flowers and birds and living creatures' that Jeffries wrote about in 1886. Statistics bear out just how full those hedgerows are. Of more than 1,700 species of plants that grow in Britain nearly a thousand have

12 The effects of Dutch elm disease

been recorded in hedgerows, though only 250 are found there more or less exclusively. About 10 million birds breed there, as do over 20 species of butterflies. Nearly half our 53 native mammals are to be found in hedgerows.

Not all the blame for this threat to wildlife habitats can fairly be laid at the farmhouse door. Hedges are also grubbed up by road builders and every other kind of developer. Dutch elm disease has robbed us of many of those hedgerow trees that are among the most gracious ornaments of our countryside (illustration 12). Oaks are being lost at the rate of about 100,000 a year, partly because improved drainage has lowered the water-table and partly by the natural process of old age and decay, though the farmer sometimes inadvertently adds to the destruction by damaging tree-roots in ploughing closer to field boundaries, as well as by careless stubble burning. His mechanical hedge-cutter, so useful in saving time and labour, unfortunately restricts regeneration by removing sapling trees that the human hedger would have spared.

Keep Britain Tidy?

On the other side of the hedge, nearly 250,000 acres of grass verges in England and Wales alone are a refuge for wildlife. For some 20 plants they are the main habitat, and for another seven the only one. Clove-scented broomrape, that curious leafless parasite, is one that grows nowhere else. Spike rampion, the less common of the two rampions, local southern plants with compound heads, is another. Blue flax, the charmingly named hare's ears, sealed cow-wheat, great hyacinth and some very unusual buttercups also rely on the verge for their home.

This richness was not understood in the 1950s by various local authorities that inflicted considerable damage on plants and mammals by using hormone weedkillers to tidy up their verges. When naturalists protested, spraying stopped in most counties, but occasional accidents still happened. One May morning in 1967 the villagers of Curbar and Froggatt, on the eastern slopes of the valley of the Derbyshire Derwent, woke to find that their road verges had changed colour overnight from deep green to rusty brown. To guard against this kind of mistake, and perhaps to atone for its earlier error, Derbyshire now has a countryside sub-committee on which the county's Naturalist Trust is represented, and similar co-operation with naturalists exists in other counties. Hereford and Worcester, for example, now has more than 30 stretches of grass verge—of up to 300yd long— designated as nature reserves.

Better news still for nature-lovers was the Department of the Environment's decision in 1975 to stop cutting grass on verges on trunk roads and motorways except in very limited circumstances, and this was backed up by a request to county councils to do the same on roads under their control. This step—in a direction signposted by both conservationist pressure and economic need—should bring back much colour and life which has been lost in the general tidying up process that has been going on in the countryside since World War II.

Tidyness is a great virtue, and when one reflects that Bank Holiday crowds visiting the National Trust's Clumber Park estate in Nottinghamshire leave behind enough litter to provide three full days' work for six men in removing it, one could wish that more people would acquire this attribute. But, like most virtues, it can lead to dullness if practised excessively. The well intentioned and generally valuable Tidy Village Competitions can sometimes lead to the destruction of wildlife habitats through a thoughtless excess of zeal. So, too, can the meticulous care of churchyards. The clearance and straightening of ditches, the substitution of piped water for farm ponds, like the use of chemical fertilisers and the destruction of hedges, may bring about more efficient farming but it makes life harder for wildlife.

Animal life under attack

That stinging nettles should be regarded as unpleasant, unsightly weeds to be disposed of on sight by farmers, gardeners and clergy may seem reasonable to those of us who have forgotten that nettles were once used as vegetables and only remember painful childhood encounters with them. It is less reasonable to the 27 species of insects which rely almost exclusively on them for food and the 17 other species which treat them as one source of a more varied diet. At least three species of butterflies, the tortoiseshell, red admiral and peacock are wholly dependent on stinging nettles, as is a fourth, the comma, in some areas. The painted lady also feeds on it, though by no means exclusively. Fortunately for them—and for us, for the disappearance of these colourful creatures would deny us of another of life's minor pleasures—stinging nettles are hard to eradicate because of their rhizomes, or stout underground storage stems. But many nettles have gone with the hedgerows, and it seems to me that these butterflies, along with others, often for rather similar reasons, are less plentiful than they used to be despite a resurgence in the hot summer of 1976. Many indeed are rare. The heath fritillary seems now to be found only in a small area in north Kent; the glanville fritillary is confined to the Isle of Wight; the lovely swallow tail is found only in the Norfolk fenland, apart from the colony that has been reintroduced to Wicken Fen in Cambridgeshire from Norfolk. But none appears to be in immediate danger of extinction, which is more than can be said of three blue butterflies, the adonis and chalk-hill blues and, particularly, the large blue.

These are all butterflies of the chalk downlands of southern England, where quite startling changes have taken place since World War II. Barley barons now challenge for authority where the sheep was undisputed king. The plough has cut deeply into the 'fine short smooth grass' that so impressed Cobbett. All the way from Gilbert White's 'mighty, majestic mountains' of Sussex to Ballard Down in Dorset, where 'the wide, wild, houseless Downes' sweep down to the cliff edge above the jagged, needle-point of Old Harry Rock, the plough is, in the words of Brian Jackman, 'laying bare the hills down to their chalk bones, stripping away the living turf and destroying its irreplaceable communities of plants, wild flowers, insects and birds'. About a quarter of Dorset's downland, including Eggardon Hill, Hamble-don Hill and stretches of coastal downs between Weymouth and Swanage, are now cultivated. On slopes too steep for the plough, beef cattle have replaced sheep, churning up the turf to leave a rough pasture on which few flowers grow. Further north, in the Chilterns, the story is much the same. With the decline of sheep and rabbits, a new cover of scrubland is creeping across Prospero's 'unshrubbed down', bringing with it new species of wildlife that may be no less interesting but will not entirely compensate for the passing of the more familiar creatures and plants.

I may be unduly alarmist about the danger to the adonis blue and the chalk-hill blue, but their dependence on the horseshoe vetch of calcareous grassland is worrying. About the threat to the large blue there is no shadow of doubt. The cards are heavily

13 Back to nature: this disused gravel pit alongside the Trent at Attenborough, Nottinghamshire, is now a nature reserve

stacked against it. For one thing, its eggs are laid on the buds of wild thyme, and Oberon would be fortunate today 'to know a bank whereon the wild thyme blows', for it is no longer the most common flower of the downs and at its present rate of decline may soon disappear altogether. For another thing, even if it finds the thyme it is still utterly dependent on two species of red ant for its life.

What happens is this. First the butterfly lays its eggs on the buds of wild thyme. The eggs hatch after about ten days of warm June sun, and the larvae start to feed upon the thyme flowers. After about three weeks the caterpillar descends from the thyme and wanders about in the grass where, if it is lucky, it may meet one of the right species of ant: either *Myrmica scabrinoides* or *M. laevonoides*. If it is unlucky, it will starve, but when by happy chance the meeting takes place, the ant caresses the honey gland of the caterpillar, enthusiastically drinking any droplets of honey. After an hour or so, the caterpillar's thoracic segments suddenly expand, whereupon the ant seizes the caterpillar between the third and fourth segments and bears it to the nest. There for six weeks in late summer and again in spring after hibernation, the ant feeds the caterpillar on its own larvae. Eventually the caterpillar matures into a white pupa, hanging by its own silk pad to the roof of the ants' nest before, as a butterfly, it crawls slowly away into the sunlight to climb up a grass stem and unfold its deep blue wings for the first time.

That was what used to happen in the Cotswolds before bulldozers tore up the breeding sites, and in Devon and north Cornwall before other breeding sites were destroyed by fires. To a limited extent—very limited in the Cotswolds—it probably still

44

happens. But the future of the large blue butterfly is precarious, which is why it is protected by the Wild Creatures and Wild Plants Conservation Act 1975.

The passing of this Act took the defence of wildlife an important step forward. Introduced as a private member's Bill by Peter Hardy, an ardent conservationist and author of a book on badgers, it not only gave legal protection to six other creatures besides the large blue and 22 species of plants all threatened with extinction but also left ajar a door through which other species could be admitted to the list by ministerial order on scientific advice. The creatures which it is now an offence 'to kill, injure or take'—in addition to the large blue—are the greater horseshoe bat, the mouse-eared bat, the smooth snake, the sand lizard and the natterjack toad.

The badger might have joined them had not strong evidence emerged that it was spreading bovine tuberculosis among cattle in Gloucestershire and adjoining counties. In the circumstances, the Bill was amended to permit the gassing under licence of suspected carriers. If some nature lovers felt that the amendment left an unjustified loophole in the Act, they had at least the satisfaction of knowing that protection against badger-digging in the name of sport was already given by the Badgers Act 1973, which soon showed it had teeth when four men in Cheshire were fined £50 each for badger-digging almost before the ink was dry on the Royal Assent. What the badger cannot be protected against is its own poor sight, and its conservative habits that take no account of electrified railways, new roads and increased traffic. Over 1,000 badgers are killed every year on the roads of Somerset alone, but the number may be slightly reduced in future thanks to the building of a special badger underpass beneath the M5 near Wellington to permit these creatures to use their ancient right of way.

The badger seems to be in no danger of extinction anyway. There may be little local difficulties in some areas, but in others he is thriving. Almost certainly, he is less threatened than the dormouse, which was also amended out of the Wild Creatures Act in the committee stage to await the outcome of a national survey by the Mammal Society.

The dormouse (illustration 14), the only British mammal that truly hibernates, may turn out to be another classic example of what happens when the countryside is tidied up. Its habitat—scrubland, hedges, coppiced deciduous woodland—is much less plentiful than it used to be and so, in consequence probably, is this charming, harmless, black-eyed, mouselike creature with squirrel tail and delightful 'Alice in Wonderland' associations. Recent reports suggest that it has vanished from Epping Forest, is very scarce in the Chilterns and south-east England but less so in Devon, though these reports may only indicate the relative alertness of naturalists in these areas in spotting this elusive creature. The best time to seek him is perhaps in late autumn when, having fattened himself on beechmast, hazel nuts or other

14 Dormouse

tree seeds, he settles down for his long winter sleep that may last six months or more and has earned him such local nicknames as dozing mouse or seven sleeper. He may be found nesting near the ground in deciduous woodlands or hazel hedges among hazel shoots or sapling stems. A very fine stripping of thin stems may indicate a nearby nest of this compact, sandy-brown creature.

Bats are also the subject of a current survey which may indicate just why these intelligent, useful insect-eaters are declining in numbers. The greater horseshoe species has been decimated. In 1951 there were believed to be about 7,000 horseshoes—so called from the shape of the hair round the nose—living in south and west England and in South Wales. Today there may be as few as 700. A quarter of these hibernate in a carefully guarded cave at the Higher Kiln Quarry nature reserve at Buckfastleigh in Devon. A local blacksmith has made two steel grilles which block the cave's two entrances to prevent unauthorised entry during the hibernation period, which usually lasts from October to March with occasional intervening periods of activity, but one grille contains a gate which allows scientists to enter the cave when the bats are absent.

A similar cave in Sussex with a grilled entrance safeguards what is thought to be the only colony of mouse-eared bats in Britain. This is not an instance of declining numbers. Although common on the continent, they were not known in this country until 1956, and their population has remained fairly static since then at something rather less than 50.

If most people regard bats as considerably less lovable than dormice, they may have even less affection for frogs and toads, whose numbers are decreasing as a result of pesticides, improved drainage and the loss of something like a third of our village ponds since 1945 through pollution, natural silting up and unnatural tidying up, while the motor car has killed many toads endeavouring to cross roads between ditch and field at the time of the spring migration. The toad, especially, has few friends among country people who cling to ancient superstitions. D. St Leger Gordon tells of a woman shopkeeper in a Dartmoor village who had no fears of being alone in her house at night but ran screaming for help at the sight of a toad in her garden in daylight. A neighbour, 'almost equally scared, shovelled the inoffensive creature into a stream at the bottom of the garden'.

Yet even the most superstitious country-dwellers must regret that the natterjack toad (illustration 15), which runs like a mouse instead of hopping, is in danger of extinction. Only a century ago it was more numerous than the common toad, but today this tiny creature of the dunes and sandy heaths seems to have vanished from most of its old sites near the east and south coasts of England between Yorkshire and Dorset, though a few colonies survive, chiefly in nature reserves. On the west coast the natterjack survives in a single habitat in Cheshire, the newly established Red Rocks Marsh nature reserve at Hoylake in the Wirral facing the mouth of the Dee, in the larger coastal

reserve between Ainsdale and Formby in Merseyside, and more numerously in Scotland along the Solway Firth and in Renfrewshire.

15 Natterjack toad

Natterjack is an inspired name for these most vocal of the frog family, better even than the more satirical 'marsh nightingale', the nickname that the loud rattling mating call of the males at night has earned for them in East Anglia, or the 'Bootle organ' by which they are known in Merseyside. Though perhaps more often heard than seen, they are visually distinguishable from common toads by the yellow stripe down their backs.

The natterjack is a skilled digger who likes to spend much of his life underground, as do the smooth snake and the sand lizard, which makes them difficult for the amateur naturalist to find. But not quite difficult enough unfortunately. One reason for the 75 per cent decline in recent years of the smooth snake and sand lizard populations—now confined to heathlands in southern England and sand dunes in Lancashire—is the acquisitiveness of man. Reptile collectors take them, advertise them in pet-trade magazines, and sell them as pets to the public, who find them friendly creatures once their initial reserve has been broken down. While the new legislation was on its way through parliament, two young men were successfully prosecuted under an earlier by-law for removing four sand lizards—as well as eight viviparous lizards—from a nature reserve on Frensham Common in Surrey, where in the last 20 years the sand lizard colonies have been reduced from 54 to 2.

Plant protection

People are indeed among the most lethal enemies of wildlife. Often the damage they inflict is unintentional. The sheer increased pressure of human beings, more mobile now in motor cars, is a threat to wildlife in all areas of Britain that attract tourists in thousands. Some damage is caused, however, by the sort of unthinking greed highlighted by the Frensham Common case. We hear of commercial florists removing rare mosses from the Peak District, an entire colony of the equally rare pasque flower being removed from a south country nature reserve, and wild flowers being uprooted in many areas by collectors, gardeners and by ignorant housewives who fancy that an unusual flower might look rather sweet in a vase in a suburban living room.

Because of this and agricultural changes and other pressures, the lady's slipper orchid, which used to grow in 20 or more sites in northern England is now confined to two or three plants on a single carefully guarded site somewhere in the Yorkshire Dales. The military orchid, at one time thought to be extinct in this country, exists still in protected nature reserves in the Chilterns and on the Rex Graham Nature Reserve near Mildenhall in Suffolk where visitors may see and photograph the flowers from a specially constructed raised path above the chalky soil that retains the heat that permits this sun-loving southern European plant to survive. For the same reason, a small version of the military orchid, called the monkey orchid because its flower is supposed to resemble the long arms of a monkey, may be found in four areas in Oxfordshire and Kent. The red helleborine lives precariously in a similar number of sites in the beechwoods of the Chilterns and the Cotswolds. That remarkable leafless flower, the ghost orchid, first recorded in 1778 as growing 'in woods between Wickham and Beaconsfield', still flowers, usually after wet springs, in the beechwoods there but nowhere else in Britain. Mezereon, which bears fragrant pink flowers in March before the leaves, is another rare plant of Chiltern beechwoods but is also found growing on the Derbyshire limestone in the Lathkill Dale National Nature Reserve.

16 Wildlife is protected in numerous National Nature Reserves, like this one in Lathkill Dale, Derbyshire

The Cheddar pink survives now in only the more inaccessible parts of the Mendips where it was once common, as do those mountain species the deep blue spring gentian in the northern Pennines and the Snowdon lily in Snowdonia.

All these are protected by the new Act, along with Alpine gentian, Alpine woodsia, Alpine sow-thistle, blue heath, diapensia, drooping saxifrage, which, like all the saxifrages, was once believed to dissolve kidney stones, the grass-like fingered sedge, Killarney fern, a moss-like small fern of western Ireland, oblong woodsia, spiked speedwell, the localised Teesdale sandwort, tufted saxifrage and the handsome, reddish-purple wild gladiolus which looks like the garden gladiolus and is found nowadays only in the New Forest.

Other flowers that have no such protection are becoming scarce. Species of marsh and wet meadows may be drained away. The fritillary, sometimes called the snakeshead because that is what it looks like, is one example. It used to grow in more than 100 localities. Now it occurs in only 13, mostly in the Thames Valley. But picking fingers are the main reason why primroses no longer herald the arrival of spring in such quantities as they once did. Their close relations, the oxlips, that Shakespeare knew, still flourish in the Cambridgeshire Naturalists' Trust's Hayley Wood and other places in eastern England, but elsewhere they are less common than they were. So too are lilies of the valley, cowslips and even bluebells, victims as much of predatory humans as of changes on the farm.

4 The Shrinking Coastline

Shifting sands

'Come unto these yellow sands,' the colourful railway station platform posters used to exhort us. To do that, preferably in the company of that frisky fisherman who informed us that Skegness was so bracing, was once the height of my ambition, taking second place only for a few weeks in December to lofty expectations of the contents of the prospective Christmas stocking. In those years of innocence before I knew the source of the quotation, I could recite by heart the name of every railway station between Bourne and Great Yarmouth and I firmly believed that the entire coast of Britain had a fringe of yellow—even golden—sands.

Now, though the pull of the coast is just as strong, the illusion, like those railway stations, has melted 'into thin air'. I know now that the sands can be clay-white in parts of Cornwall, muddy-grey round our estuaries, coal-black in County Durham or invisible below motor car bodies in several places. I have discovered that of nearly 6,000 miles of coastline round Britain, we have made a fairly successful attempt to ruin nearly three quarters of it.

Much of the damage was done before those slightly misleading posters were slapped on to the hoardings. The colliery proprietors of Durham were spilling their coal waste on the beaches, the iron-masters had built their gaunt works on the cliffs at Skinningrove, and resorts were pumping untreated sewage into the sea, as 95 of them still do, long before John Hassall conceived his jolly fisherman of Skegness. The springy, sheep-shaven turf of the Sussex Downs still rolled up to the cliff edge between Saltdean and Newhaven until 1915 when a development company decided to build a planned town called New Anzac-on-Sea which degenerated into that prototype of seaside subtopia now called Peacehaven.

The National Trust's 'Enterprise Neptune', launched in the 1960s did, and is still doing, much to arrest and even reverse the attack on our coastline from within, but so far, not enough. Nearly all the pressures that threaten our countryside—and a few more besides—endanger our yellow sands.

The natural erosion that I mentioned in the first chapter is an obvious danger that can be contained by skilled engineers provided they have the money to play with. The less obvious danger of erosion by too many human feet, wearing the turf down to bed-rock at places like Land's End and Kynance Cove and nearly as badly on the west side of Lulworth Cove, has now been identified and is being—or will be—dealt with in a manner similar to the method I have already described for inland areas.

Saving our sand dunes is more difficult. For one reason, sand dune erosion can be hard to spot. For another, it can develop quickly. A 30ft high sand dune system can vanish in a month. Replacing it will take two years, with another 4 years to wait before it is fully stabilised.

Several medieval settlements and a once-important anchorage for Ireland-bound shipping lie buried under one of Britain's most extensive dune-systems, Newborough Warren, on the south-eastern shores of Anglesey. A government instruction to the mayor of Newborough in 1561 to prevent the cutting of marram grass for use in mat-making helps to explain the restlessness of the Newborough dunes. The planting of marram grass still goes on there, but no longer because of the activities of the mat-makers. The main enemy now, apart from the cruel sea and the burrowing rabbits, is the general public who come to Anglesey in numbers that increase by about ten per cent each year. Among these are artists and photographers to whom the view of Snowdonia across the yellow and green foreground of sand and marram grass, and the blue middle ground of the Menai Straits, is irresistible. Many others are amateur naturalists who come to admire the grass of Parnassus, felwort marsh orchid and the rare marsh and dune helleborine that grow in the damp troughs, called dune slacks, lying between the ridges. These explain why the Warren is now a National Nature Reserve.

In winter, when the last of these visitors has left, workers of the Forestry Commission, who have planted conifers over large sections of the Warren, set to work to repair the ravages of summer and restore stability to the dunes. Without this vigilance, roads, car parks and even forest plantations in this fascinating

17 Creeping sand dunes threaten to engulf this ancient church at Llandanwg, North Wales

51

corner of Britain would soon lie buried under sand as the road behind the Ainsdale–Southport dunes in Merseyside has been buried several times in recent years.

The dune spit called East Head, which is the western tip of Selsey Bill but the eastern headland of Chichester Harbour, almost vanished into the sea in the early 1960s, but now seems to be safe for the immediate future thanks to a desperate and costly rescue operation by the local authority and various voluntary bodies. This splendid combined operation came too late to prevent the extinction through sheer pressure of human feet of what had been the most easterly habitat in Britain of the Portland spurge, but just in time to save the Mediterranean sea heath and a most unusual invertebrate fauna.

A rather similar operation has been in progress for several years in Northumberland to save the lovely sweep of dunes that separate those two massive castle-topped outcrops of blue-grey igneous rock called the Whin Sill at Bamburgh and Dunstanburgh. That some restoration might be necessary became apparent in the late 1960s when increasing numbers of tourists who had previously ignored Northumberland as a county of cold east winds, incomprehensible accents and heavy industry began to find that though the winds could be cool and the dialect difficult to southern ears, native hearts were warm, industry was confined to a comparatively small south-eastern triangle of an otherwise astonishingly empty county and that the beaches, like the romantic castles behind them, were superb. With the completion since then of the Tyne tunnel and the Alnwick by-pass, which allowed motorists to dodge such impediments as Newcastle's Tyne Bridge, the main streets of Morpeth and the needle-eyed Hotspur Gate at Alnwick, the need became urgent as motorists parked on the edges of dunes and then spilled out their occupants to laze or picnic in the slacks while their children rolled down the steep slopes. The result was nearly disastrous. In places the grass roots were exposed— and died. There were minor blow outs. Fortunately, thanks to a local press campaign, volunteers backed by the National Trust, which owns some of the best bits, saved the dunes, for the time being at least. Wherever there are dunes there are latent dangers, but fortunately, because of its geographical position, the Northumberland coast is never likely to be overwhelmed with visitors.

Suburban seaside

It is still possible, despite those new by-passes, to walk along the beach in Beadnell Bay on a mid-morning in high summer and return two hours later in your own footprints. This is more than you dare do at places like Brean in Somerset, Black Rock in Gwynedd and Pendine in Gwent where motorists are allowed to park on the beaches. There is nothing new about this; Sir Malcolm Campbell scurried up and down Pendine Sands breaking world land speed records between 1924 and 1927. But

18　Motor mania is virtually taking over the beaches too

in those days cars were thin on the ground—even thinner on the sands. Today more than 500,000 people live within an hour's drive of Pendine and 3 times as many within 2 hours' drive. Tomorrow, or in ten years' time there will be more still and when you think of it you wonder if it will then be possible to see any sand between the cars.

By then, though, much of our coastline may be obscured by caravans, chalets and 'Cosy Cots', those 'desirable residences' flung up by speculative builders around our coasts. These three threats to our enjoyment of our coastline are closely related, all products of the motor car age and of increasing affluence. But as the seaside-villa culture was the first to arrive it must be dealt with first.

More than 70 years ago E. V. Lucas called Brighton 'a suburb, a lung of London'. It was the railways that made possible that first extension of suburbia to the sea, but it was the development of the internal combustion engine that enabled the lung to expand between the wars in a long ribbon of brick that stretched over most of the Sussex coast and, for that matter, along the Hampshire coast as well, so that today Portsmouth and Southampton almost merge in a straggling Solent city. Further west there is virtually no gap in the brick and concrete jungle between Milford on Sea and Poole in the greater Bournemouth which vies with the Sussex coast for the title of 'Costa Geriatrica', so great is its attraction for the well heeled retired. A similar title, with a Lancashire accent, could be given to that elongated townscape that stretches from Lytham, where the accent is less marked, through Blackpool to Fleetwood.

'What's done, cannot be undone,' as Lady Macbeth put it so succinctly, and you may say there is no point in recalling battles to save areas that were lost long ago. But if the major battles have been lost in these areas, minor skirmishes are still being fought to save patches of fine country that survived the earlier holocaust. Such an engagement is being fought as I write over more than 17 acres of still unspoiled hill and headland overlooking Newhaven Harbour in Sussex. The local council sold this land and the impressive fort that stands on part of it in the 1960s despite public protest. Outline permission has been given for development. Another bit of coastal Britain may vanish almost unnoticed except by local people who care. Is so small an area of land and a redundant fort worth fighting to retain in an area that has already lost so much? The answer is surely that we must fight to retain every inch of unspoilt coastline and fight doubly hard where there is so little left to save.

Whether the ribbons of villas are more or less depressing than their poor relations of shacks and chalets and seaside shanty towns is a matter for individual taste. The chalets that seem to grow out of the cliffs behind the long pebble beach at Branscombe, between Beer and Seaton in South Devon, blend better with their surroundings than many more pretentious buildings along the cliff-tops. There are others along the coasts of Lincolnshire and what is now Humberside that I would be prepared to defend because they are uncluttered and add a touch of gaiety and colour to what can be a rather melancholy coastline. But it is difficult to say anything favourable of Jaywick or Canvey Island in Essex, East Wittering in Sussex, Heacham and Snettisham on the Norfolk shore of the Wash, or of that vast shack colony that stretches along the Clwyd coast between Point of Air and Abergele. They date in the main from the 1930s, with post-war additions. Largely deserted in the winter, these shack towns presumably give pleasure and a taste of sea air to their inhabitants in the summer. They certainly add nothing to the beauty of our coast, and we must see to it that they spread no further.

That the static chalet is now less popular than the technically mobile caravan which is attracted to these shanty towns like ants to a picnic makes little difference to the quality of the scenery; a clutter of each is equally devastating. I am thinking now of the caravans that remain seemingly anchored in one place from Easter to October. The genuinely mobile caravan often belongs to someone who is passionately seeking solitude, as well as an escape from soaring hotel prices, and if his is the solitary van in a field it does little to mar the scenery. The more gregarious caravanner is likely to belong to the Caravan Club, which usually goes to some trouble to find unobtrusive sites. Obviously there is going to come a time—perhaps before long—when mobile caravans will be a menace. But meanwhile, except to other motorists when in transit, they are less harmful than the static variety which threatens to swamp the Welsh coast in particular.

I am not too worried that Porthcawl has the largest caravan park in Europe, because Porthcawl's main appeal has never been its beauty. Nor am I unduly disturbed to discover that

Abergele has 30 times more caravan and chalet accommodation than it has hotel or boarding house rooms, because it is far too late to do anything about Abergele beyond avoiding it. But I am sorry that Newquay, in what used to be Cardiganshire, now Dyfed, is almost engulfed by caravans, because its charm lies in its white, Georgian houses that tell of a quietly distinguished past as a seaport and ship-building town. Though Mrs Ogmore-Pritchard, whom Dylan Thomas introduced in *Early One Morning* when he lived in Newquay, might have accepted the yachts that now enliven the harbour she would have sniffed audibly but genteely at the mention of caravans. I am concerned, too, that Towyn, just south of the Dovey, is all but encircled by caravans, because the Towyn I knew was a Victorian period-piece seaside resort. And I wonder how long Anglesey is going to take an annual increase of around ten per cent in its caravan population before the 'island full' signs go up. Most of all I am worried about the Lleyn Peninsula.

Why Lleyn? You may well ask, for this muscular leg of North Wales that paddles out for 32 miles into the Irish Sea is surely one of the least spoilt parts of the principality. Apart from some dramatic quarrying near the north-west coast, little harm has so far come to Lleyn. There is, it is true, a large holiday camp at Pen-ychain, between Criccieth and Pwllheli, but this isolated

19 Contrast the peace of this rural coastline, near St David's, Pembrokeshire, with the urban development of illustration 20

temple to whoever is the goddess of escapism is very much an island unto itself that seems neither to notice the rest of the Peninsula nor to be noticed by it. Otherwise, Lleyn is a green and pleasant land of hummocky fields and rugged farms; a secret land criss-crossed by steep, twisting, aimless lanes that sometimes lead to rugged headlands and steep tracks that hurry on down to hidden, sheltered, uncluttered sands, and sometimes to vantage points that give breath-taking views, like that from Rhiw across the wide empty bay of Porth Neigwl (which the tourists call Hell's Mouth), or from the swollen big toe of Lleyn across to Bardsey Island, once the goal of pilgrims in search of absolution and now of naturalists in search of rare birds.

This, as I say, is a secret land. That some of the inhabitants want to preserve its secrecy is evident from the armless or defaced signposts and from the way that caravans are moved on from Criccieth as vagrants were moved on from parishes in Tudor times. But the caravans are infiltrating into the Peninsula. Llanbedrog and Abersoch have not yet gone the way of Abergele, or even Newquay, but the danger signs are there. Some of the beaches are being discovered. There is a shop, and the inevitable attendant litter, on the beach at Porthor Oer, or Whistling Sands, where the sand squeaks under your feet. The Lleyn Peninsula is a long way from being spoilt, because it is a long way from the big towns and the main tourist routes. But its future needs careful watching. 'It's changing', a visitor to Llanbedrog told me, 'I've been coming here for 20 years and I've noticed it becoming more commercialised each year.'

The same could be said of Wells-next-the-Sea in Norfolk and Seahouses in Northumberland. They are small towns or large villages some 200 miles apart on England's east coast but curiously alike in some ways and sharing a similar uncertainty about their future role. Both are delightful places to spend a relaxing holiday, but both have real working lives of their own that make them more interesting than the contrived 'resorts' that hibernate when the last visitor has left.

Wells is an ancient sea-port. Today it is the only surviving commercial port along a 70-mile stretch of coast between the Wash and Great Yarmouth, the increased size of ships and the silting up of harbours having closed its old rivals Blakeney, Cley and Wiveton to all but sailing dinghies. A quayside inn called 'The Fleece' hints broadly at far-off days when ships went scurrying to and fro across the North Sea with cargoes of wool from the backs of the thick-coated Marshland sheep. Coastal cargo vessels still feel their way over the sand-bar and down the long, shallow channel into Wells, but the chief trade of the harbour is in fish, chiefly in sprats—'roka' is the local word—or whelks, which are unloaded straight into coppers in quayside boiling-sheds before dispatch to shops and stalls all over Britain.

Compared with Wells, Seahouses was a late developer. It began life in the mid-nineteenth century as a seaward extension of North Sunderland, a rather grim-looking village a mile or

so inland. The houses by the sea from which the village acquired its name were built to shelter men working in the new harbour that served North Sunderland's export trade in lime. Lime-kilns still stand on the quayside, but now house fishing-tackle, for as the lime trade declined the fishing industry developed. Today the impressive harbour is just as busy as Wells'. To both places the movement of boats, the unloading of fish and the salty talk of fishermen give a tang of reality that is missing from those nineteenth-century products of the discovery that the sea just beyond a new railway terminus was enjoyable for splashing about in or for observing decorously from some esplanade garden or newly constructed pier.

Because Wells is a product of spontaneous, piecemeal growth, it has what John Seymour, who knows it well, has called 'one of the most distinguished water-fronts in England'. To appreciate that to the full you have to walk seawards along the mile-long bank that runs parallel to the harbour approach channel, and then look back. What you see is a compact little town of colourful buildings that end abruptly where the fields begin on either side. There are no blurred edges of new development. Along the waterfront are the splendid eighteenth- and nineteenth-century warehouses and inns. Even a coaling wharf and an immense early twentieth-century grain-storage warehouse blend effectively from that distance. Behind the town, rising above pantiled roofs, is the splendid tower of the parish church.

Seahouses cannot compete with this. It has no such viewpoint for one thing. It is mainly Victorian or later for another. But from the end of its quay it offers a satisfying view of a huddle of buildings climbing up from the harbour and then a line of fairly modern hotels stretching out narrow fingers towards the dunes of Bamburgh on one side and Beadnell on the other. The backcloth of Cheviot foothills behind the town, with the splendid pile of Bamburgh Castle on one wing and ruined Dunstanburgh on the other add a note of drama that is missing from Wells.

In their slightly different ways, Wells and Seahouses are jewels to be carefully guarded. Unfortunately, there has already been some chipping away of these precious gems. The caravans already rest in these little towns and with the caravan parks, as so often happens, have come the beginnings of the bingo, chips and candy-floss sub-culture.

At Wells the sub-culture is more offensive than the caravan park, which is well screened behind the dunes, invisible from the beach and almost so from most parts of the town. It is also well run as, to be fair, are the bingo and fruit-machine palaces. In Southend or Cleethorpes, where you expect that sort of thing, they would doubtless be regarded as models of their kind. But on that splendid quayside at Wells they fit as uneasily as a pop group in the Vatican.

So does the miscellaneous collection of caravans that occupies the best site in Seahouses, right at the heart of the little town, facing the harbour approach. The amusements are rather less obtrusive, except when a breeze from the wrong quarter brings the pungent scent of fried chips to the nose.

In neither place is the harm irreparable. The danger lies ahead. There has already been talk of building a large amusement complex at Seahouses. Somebody should say now that enough is enough.

Wells and Seahouses occupy sensitive positions in areas that are among the most interesting and unspoilt stretches of coast in Britain. Both areas pride themselves on their enlightened attitudes to conservation. The north Norfolk coast has ten nature reserves between Snettisham and Weybourne, including two of national status. The National Trust owns land on either side of both Wells and Seahouses. They are probably fully aware of the possible weaknesses in otherwise unguarded spots. I hope the local authorities concerned are equally awake. If either place develops illusions of becoming an East-coast Blackpool the result would be disastrous.

Offshore oil

Some areas rely so heavily on their sense of isolation and remoteness that it takes only a few extra motor cars and additional caravans to ruin the whole atmosphere. This is true of the Lleyn Peninsula, of north Norfolk and of Northumberland. So it is of the north coast of Scotland between Cape Wrath and Duncansby Head, facing that cruellest of all seas, the Pentland Firth, where a galloping tide pressing against a gale of wind can set up tumultuous seas that make sailors yearn, like the 'good Gonzalo', for 'an acre of barren ground, long heath, brown furze, any thing'.

Tourists go in their shoals to John O' Groats to gaze across this foaming expanse of sea and to be able to boast that they have gone as far north as is possible on the mainland of Britain. Fewer go to Cape Wrath, because it involves a ferry-crossing of the Kyle of Durness and a ten-mile minibus ride over tortuous roads and a ford, and so miss the more dramatic view, from the lighthouse on the end of a 523ft cliff, which can extend on a clear day to Lewis, 40 miles away, and even the Ward Hill of Hoy, 60 miles away to the north east. Even so, some 15,000 tourists a year make their way to what could well be the least accessible place on the mainland of Britain. Many more now visit the splendidly varied coastline between these two points. Lots of them go with their houses towed behind them and cameras at the ready to snap the great colonies of birds— kittiwakes, razorbills, guillemots and an increasing number of fulmar petrels—that nest among the rocks on such places as the 700ft high cliffs of Torridonian sandstone at Clo Mor in Sutherland and the slightly lower headlands of Dunnet and Duncansby in Caithness, or such waders as the ringed plover and the oystercatcher of the shores and estuaries, and the several varieties of terns that nest more vulnerably in the dunes.

Now, though, a greater danger than a growing army of tourists threatens the hitherto remote Scottish coastline. Offshore oil may bring prosperity to Scotland and solve some of Britain's balance-of-payment worries, but it may also drive away the colonies of seabirds and banish the beauty that so much of Scotland's coast wears like a cloak.

So far (1976), except for the use of Scrabster as a service base, nothing has happened to the northern coast, and nothing disastrous to the environment of the west or east coasts. Aberdeen's hotel bedrooms may be full and its house prices soaring above London levels, but it has kept its feet on the ground and it remains one of the most civilised, attractive and unspoilt of all Britain's cities. Across on the lovely, mountainous coast of Wester Ross, the tiny village of Drumbuie, near the entrance to Loch Carron, has narrowly escaped becoming a centre for the building of oil-production platforms.

This was a notable triumph for the conservationists, but they had barely finished congratulating themselves when, a month later, permission was given to build platforms on the nearby shores of Loch Kishorn. The stone for the site is being taken from two new quarries, one on the Isle of Skye and the other from Strathcarron at the eastern end of Loch Carron. This has detracted somewhat from what a local minister in the last century described as 'a scene of rural felicity and of rural beauty . . .' though so far, it must be said, both projects are dwarfed into insignificance by the towering backdrop of mountains behind them.

Across on the east coast, where the terrain is flatter and lusher, the changes show up more starkly, and not only visually. When oilmen in the pubs of Nigg Bay speak of spuds they are using the technological jargon of their trade and not discussing the potatoes which are the staple product of the local crofts.

21 This caravan site in the Pembrokeshire National Park is less obtrusive than many which are threatening to spread all along our coastline

In the islands, too, a way of life is changing. Sullom Voe in the Shetlands has already been marked down to become what journalists have christened the 'Rotterdam of the North'. On Flotta, one of the more remote of the Orkney isles, the incoming oilmen already outnumber the indigenous population by eight to one. In Stornoway, capital of Lewis, where every other person seems to be a McLeod and every other male a Roddy McLeod, the oil magnate may do what Lord Leverhulme failed to do half a century ago and revolutionise the town's economy. That in itself is perhaps no bad thing. It is what may go with it which is to be feared: the scars on the landscape, the loss of that almost mystical Hebridean atmosphere. The road to the isles may soon be paved with black gold, but oil is slippery and there could be disastrous falls.

It seems inevitable that the islands as we knew them will vanish completely. Indeed, the character of much of the Scottish mainland will change. The time to see the Highlands and the Islands is now, before it is too late.

That might be said, too, of Pembrokeshire. Its lovely coast, already encroached upon by the military, may be endangered by oil strikes in what has mysteriously become the 'Celtic Sea'. Pembroke Dock and Milford Haven are already developing into large oil ports. Any major oil find might threaten the walled town of Tenby or the almost Trollopean calm of that mini-cathedral city of St Davids. Oil-rig platforms that may look small in a Highland setting would utterly disfigure the small-scale scenery of Pembrokeshire.

Nor is the threat confined to the scenery. Oil pollution already takes a heavy toll of wildlife, especially of sea birds, like the auk and various sea duck. Over 1,000 eider ducks died in an oiling incident in the Tay estuary in 1968. A similar incident could destroy 95 per cent of that diving duck, the scaup, which winters in the Firth of Forth off Leith. The oil companies are equipped to deal with the minor spillages that inevitably occur, but the danger of another *Torrey Canyon* disaster is never far from the minds of nature-lovers round Lynas Point in Anglesey, where tankers moor to discharge oil direct into an underwater pipe-line. Such dangers are bound to increase as the off-shore oil industry develops, but more harm comes at present from minor spillages, either by accident or sheer carelessness, from oil-burning merchant ships.

Oil is not the only danger. Discharge from the rapidly growing chemical industry is now causing increasing pollution in the Severn and Humber estuaries, as well as from such rivers as the Mersey and Ribble, which could create trouble among the mallard that winter in such vast numbers on those wide sands of Morecambe Bay. Just a little further to the north, on that undervalued, quiet Lakeland coast, radio-active waste from Windscale is seeping into the sea, though not, the experts say soothingly, in sufficient quantities to harm either humans or wildlife. But you cannot help wondering, just as you wonder about the effects of the warm water discharged from new power stations round our coasts. Again, the effects may not be harmful, but the warmer water is bound to create a changed habitat for wildlife.

The biggest problem that faces the future of our coastline is, as inland, the whittling away of space. It has been estimated that there are four square inches of seashore available for every man, woman and child in Britain. New development of every kind is steadily reducing even that small amount, though if you go down to the desolate shores of the Wash or Foulness in winter you wonder about the accuracy of the calculations.

At Foulness, where land and sea merge in a vast expanse of level emptiness, you seem to have come to the end of the world. For how long, nobody seems to know. The Maplin airport project has been abandoned. About the proposed seaport, nothing is being said—yet. Some time, perhaps before long, Foulness will cease to be an infinity of dunes, mud and sea. Will it matter? Foulness is not really a beautiful area. There are shacks and caravan parks and service stations and a top-secret Ministry of Defence establishment, and just an occasional pretty village like Paglesham. It is a sort of Thorne Moor by the sea, and you can become addicted to it in the same sort of way. If its character changes, there will be those who will miss it, if only for the sake of the melancholy cries of those vast colonies of brent geese that wheel around in the wide winter skies.

5 Towns in Trouble

Travelling around Britain, you sometimes get the impression that the only towns not in the process of destroying themselves have already achieved maximum devastation or are about to start on the road to ruin. It may be a false impression; a few towns have planned wisely; some have even let well almost alone, but the majority, erroneously believing that trendiness is next to godliness, have blindly followed the blind in replacing their varied regional characters with a dull uniformity.

This is not an entirely novel situation. About once a century since the Great Rebuilding of 1560–1640, most of our cities and towns have felt an urgent need for a face-lift, and have re-modelled themselves, which explains why many a Tudor or Jacobean building is masked by a Georgian or Victorian façade.

Canterbury

Victorian local authorities were no more sensitive than their successors about removing good buildings that stood in the way of what they considered to be progress. Canterbury achieved everlasting notoriety by selling its castle to the Gas, Light and Coke Company, allowing St Augustine's Abbey ruins to become a beer garden and demolishing all its medieval gates except one, though it did later strike a light tap—rather than a blow—for conservation by refusing a circus proprietor's request to demolish the sole surviving gate—West Gate—to permit the passage of his animal cages. But no objection was offered at the removal of two large prehistoric mounds to permit the building of Canterbury's East Station. The Suffolk town of Clare allowed its railway station to be built inside the confines of its castle mound, and Leicester, among other places, permitted the railway to scythe through its heart, though the trail of demolition was confined to a narrow swath. Some towns, like Northampton and Derby, firmly kept the railways in their places—on the outskirts. Certainly no local authority sold its soul to the steam engine as some modern ones have to the internal combustion engine. The pressures from transport and commercial interests were generally less than they are today, and the scale of urban redevelopment—apart from Canterbury and a few other black spots—much smaller.

Fortunately, many of our most notably historic towns have withstood the mid-twentieth-century pressures reasonably well. Even Canterbury still has a surprisingly large number of handsome old buildings that have survived not only the nineteenth-century 'improvers' but the greater vandalism of the June blitz in 1942 that mangled one third of the area within the city walls. Unscarred by both attacks, the cathedral still rises majestically above a city now firmly committed to conservation but just a little apprehensive that future efforts to ease its traffic problems might do further harm to the environment. Much the same could be said of York, which carries its years rather more lightly. Now that its glorious Minster has been

22 Despite Victorian vandalism and Baedeker blitzes, Mercery Street, Canterbury, retains its medieval width and tone

63

saved and the eastern end of the precincts cleared of its clutter of parked cars, the city looks more handsome than ever.

Chester and Edinburgh

Chester was fortunate. Chosen by the Council of Europe as the site for one of England's pilot projects for Architectural Heritage Year in 1975, it had extra cash from the government to help it on its way, a fact which must have aroused pangs of envy in other cities, especially in Edinburgh, which needs to tackle the same sort of job before long.

There is no need to panic about Edinburgh. It is still one of the most exciting cities to visit in all Europe. It still has something like 50,000 individual buildings listed of architectural or historic interest. But occasionally one or two disappear. Too many of the others are beginning to look shabby. Bits of the Old Town south of the Royal Mile have been nibbled away by a ring-road and an expanding university; others may follow. The Royal Mile itself has a sprinkling of medieval buildings that cry out for restoration before it is too late. Some are empty and showing signs of decay. Even in the New Town, some once-noble Georgian houses are taking on a pinched and hungry look. You get the feeling that Edinburgh, dozing, has neglected the early warning signs of approaching decline. If only the whole city centre had been made a conservation area, as happened at Chester, the situation might have been different. As it is, Edinburgh has awakened to the dangers at last, but only to find that money is scarce. There is no danger of the castle sliding down into Princes Street gardens, or any other major disaster, but if you have never seen Edinburgh, try to go there fairly soon—just in case.

Bath

Intending visitors to Bath should take similar advice. In fact the best time to visit Bath was yesterday, or, better still, 30 years ago. Nobody quite knows how many good, mainly Georgian, buildings Bath has lost since World War II, because most were listed 'Grade III' and could be demolished without notifying Whitehall, but it has been estimated at nearly 20,000. That figure should be seen in perspective. Bath is still the nearest thing we have in Britain to a complete Georgian city. Only it is not quite as near as it was. Something like 15 per cent of its Georgian buildings have vanished, mostly from the outer fringes, because Bath made the same mistake as Edinburgh in putting its finest groups of buildings into separate conservation areas instead of treating the city as a whole and making it one vast conservation area. The pace of demolition has slowed down since it created a national outcry in the early 1970s, but it has not entirely stopped.

Nor is it Bath's only problem. Its streets, planned to take sedan chairs with some degree of comfort, are hardly suited to the motor car age. A by-pass is needed, as everyone agrees. But hardly anyone seems to agree about where it should go without harming the city or its setting. Through and partly under the heart of the city, as Sir Colin Buchanan suggests, seemed to many people a poor solution. The debate continues, not always conducted with the 'gallantry and levity' that Defoe thought to be characteristic of Bath, and may do so for years to come.

Eventually, I suppose, a solution will be found; must be found. Bath is a national treasure that must not be squandered. It has so much to offer that its self-inflicted scars hardly show yet. The Royal Crescent still sweeps graciously round its shelf on the Mendip slopes (illustration 23); the Abbey, for all its clutter of memorial plaques to those who served their country in the farthest flung outposts of Empire, is still a noble building; Robert Adam's Pulteney Bridge remains the most beautiful bridge in Britain; though it would be seen to greater advantage if closed to traffic; ladies who are sisters under the skin to Jane Austen's contemporaries still tinkle tea-spoons in the Pump Room above the baths in which Roman legionaries once splashed. In Bath it is still possible to day-dream yourself back into the elegant eighteenth century of Beau Nash. But just occasionally, your reverie is disturbed by the crash of falling masonry or the strident bleep of an urgent hooter.

Chichester

So it is in Chichester, though as I write there are no bleeps round the Market Cross in the heart of the city, where North, South, East and West Streets meet. This central core now forms a delightful traffic-free enclave where one can sit, continental

23 A perfect example of Georgian architecture, Bath's Royal Crescent survives in a city beset by crises

fashion, on seats in the middle of what used to be some of the busiest town streets in south-eastern England. But this peace has been bought at a cost. Some charming buildings have been swept away to provide alternative streets fit for motorists to drive in, and some of the new buildings that have gone up lately around the city have decidely lacked charm. Chichester needs to decide very soon whether it wants more of these monstrosities and whether its traffic scheme, which is still experimental, should be made permanent.

Winchester

Winchester too is wracked by Hamlet-like indecision. It shares with Bath, if less acutely, a traffic problem, symbolised, as Leslie Ginsburg and Kenneth Brown put it so aptly in *Architectural Review* (November 1975), by 'King Alfred, imprisoned on his roundabout opposite Guildhall at the foot of High Street'. Winchester also has doubts about its future role. Whether to remain a county town, educational centre, shopping centre for the surrounding Itchen Valley villages, with some tourism attracted by Britain's longest cathedral and a wealth of literary and historical associations, or to branch out as an ambitious commercial and shopping centre, that is the question.

Of course, the two problems are closely linked. If Winchester goes for growth it will need to be dressed in the panoply of ring-roads, M3 links, the lot. But is this its best option? Is the city big enough to compete with growing Basingstoke and an out-of-town shopping centre at Chandler's Ford? Is it the right place for department stores? Ginsburg and Brown think not; I agree. It perhaps needs more specialist shops and a good art gallery and museum, as they suggest. It probably does not need its proposed ring-road (three quarters of a ring to be precise), about which the local authority, under pressure from local conservationists, is having second thoughts.

Much of the post-war development in Winchester seems to have been designed for an expanding jet-age city, as does some of the 'unbuilding'—those vast Siberian-desert-like car parks. The development looks out of proportion somehow in what is essentially a market town in a rural setting, with a view of the wooded slopes of St Catherine's Hill from the end of nearly every street. The real Winchester of King Alfred and Jane Austen is to be found by the mill-streams and riverside walks below the Guildhall, or in the wonderfully restful green precincts of the cathedral, the calm heart of the city, or even in the suburbs so full of good buildings and so much part of the city in a way that suburbs of bigger cities rarely are. Almost the last building in Winchester, if you leave it along the Southampton Road, is St Cross Hospital, the finest medieval almshouse still standing in Britain. There you can still demand and receive the Wayfarers' Dole of ale and bread. Standing there, sipping your ale and gazing out across the Itchen water-meadows, you find yourself praying silently that Winchester will always stay this way; not standing still, of course, because no place can do that, but adapting itself gradually to change, and taking with it into the future the best of the past.

Gloucester and Worcester

I am not sure that either of those neighbouring cathedral cities of Gloucester and Worcester have managed this gradual adaptation without scars. Of the two, Gloucester seems to be faring the worse. Its cathedral is magnificent. The fan vaulting in its cloisters inspired the similar work in Westminster Abbey and St George's Chapel, Windsor. But the number of other historic buildings in the city seems pitifully small and becoming depressingly smaller. There is an excellent sixteenth-century timber framed building in Westgate Street that houses a fine folk museum, and three or four others of similiar vintage. One of them, a superb Elizabethan farmhouse on the site of the ruins of Llanthony Priory, was being used as a dumping ground by a scrap merchant until the city council bought it in 1974. It will be restored when there is spare money in the kitty—if it does not fall down first. I am not suggesting that Gloucester's council would deliberately allow that to happen, but I know of ancient buildings in other towns that have been studiously neglected until the demolition men have had to be called in to perform the last rites to the accompaniment of mournful dirges on the theme of excessive costs of restoration and crocodile sobs from the local Town Hall.

Though I doubt very much if the city fathers of Worcester are aiming at that sort of situation—they got into enough hot water in the 1960s—they will be in trouble again if something is not done soon about Bridge Street. This is a street of good, solid Georgian brick houses, none individually memorable but nearly all with handsome porches and fanlights above the front doors, and all helping to make up a street scene of dignity and character. Some of the dignity has already gone because most of the buildings look seedy, or did when I was there in April 1975. It so happened that the Duke of Grafton, chairman of the Society for the Protection of Ancient Buildings, had mentioned Bridge Street in a speech in Thomas White's magnificent Worcester Guildhall only the previous week. 'I am extremely worried about the present appearance of Bridge Street,' he had said, according to *Berrow's Worcester Journal*, which, incidentally, is Britain's oldest newspaper, just a bit older than either the Guildhall of 1722 or the Bridge Street houses. 'Every other property seems to be empty and in disrepair,' he had told his Civic Society audience, and appealed to them, 'Don't let Bridge Street go.'

I hope the advice will be heeded because apart from its intrinsic worth, Bridge Street holds an important strategic position leading to the bridge which the Hon John Byng, that inveterate, irascible traveller, saw under construction in 1781 and is now a notorious traffic bottleneck, and then continues on to the county cricket ground. This ground somehow symbolises

24 Sadly now demolished, the Doric façade of Ivanhoe Baths (1822), once a relic of Ashby-de-la-Zouch's former importance as a spa

Worcester, offering from one side of the pitch a perfect view of the glorious cathedral tower on its bank above the Severn, and on the other a drab view of a wartime power station. That is the essential Worcester: a strange mixture of good buildings and bad, old buildings and new (and not all the new buildings are bad). The voice of public opinion snarled just in time to stop the 'Sack' from being complete. Worcester is still worth seeing, especially the cathedral, but its future will need watching.

Lincoln

The same thing can be said, more forcibly, about Lincoln. Of course Lincoln is still very much worth a visit. When you approach from the west along the Fosse Way, that once echoed the tramp of marching Roman legionaries, you see the magnificent central tower of the cathedral perched high on its limestone plateau above the levels of the Witham valley. For grandeur of setting, Durham alone among the cathedrals of Britain can compete. Architecturally, it has no equal, in the eyes of some experts, including Alec Clifton-Taylor, who rhapsodised it in the television series *Spirit of the Age*. He attributes the pre-eminence of Lincoln to its unity of style, the result of an almost total rebuilding in the Early English manner after earlier buildings had been destroyed by fire and earthquake.

Something almost as devastating as an earthquake struck the city of Lincoln between 1968 and 1973. In those 5 years, 21 listed buildings were razed to the ground, almost the same number as had vanished in the previous 20 years. The 13 that were demolished in 1973 represented almost 10 per cent of all the listed buildings that disappeared from the face of Britain in that single year. For a city of 75,000 people this amounted to a holocaust no less wanton than the 'Sack of Worcester', but it passed almost unnoticed until a party of Inspectors of Historic Buildings for the Department of the Environment travelled to Lincoln especially to see a particularly fine example of industrial

68

architecture called Dickinson's Mill, and found it had gone, demolished on the council's authority without permission from the Department.

That was when the demolition had to stop. A reorganisation of the city's administration around the same time brought a change of heart. The Roman wall, parts of which were threatened by the city's development programme, has now been saved. Since 1974 no planning permission has been given for the removal of a single listed building; an inner ring-road scheme has been dropped, the main conservation area has been extended downhill to the railway line that separates the old Lincoln from the new.

So Lincoln still has many old buildings to see: Newport Arch in the Roman wall; two of the few surviving twelfth-century dwellings left in Britain, the Jew's house and Aaron's house, close together on the steep hill that drops to the Stonebow; the Guildhall above it like a parvise above a church porch; and High Bridge lined with shops like old London Bridge. But you can't help regretting those 40 and more buildings that you can no longer see, and though it looks as if the local authority has seen the light, it would be wise not to postpone a trip to Lincoln, just in case another earthquake should strike the city.

Peterborough and Carlisle

It might be as well to take in Peterborough while you are over in the eastern counties, which makes an early visit essential, for Peterborough is in the throes of a metamorphosis that will change it from an old town to a New Town, trebling its population to about 180,000. Not many tourists think of going to Peterborough anyway. It tends to be regarded as purely a railway and engineering centre which, though broadly true, overlooks the presence of a splendid cathedral in the local Barnack stone with one of England's most impressive west fronts. Other- wise, apart from the Guildhall of 1641, with its steep gable and hipped roof, the church of St John the Baptist, dating from 1402, and a few good Georgian houses, it is something of an architectural desert. But it has one pleasant oasis that is in danger of being drained to make way for a new Queen Street shopping centre. There is nothing especially memorable about the 15 buildings that are likely to go, except perhaps for a row of almshouses and an eighteenth-century hotel, but they form together an attractive reminder of Peterborough's past. Though local conservationists are fighting to keep them, the chances of success are probably not bright in a city that has its eyes firmly fixed on the future. But it seems to me that a modern industrial centre needs to hang on to some reminders of its past, just to keep things in perspective, which is exactly what Carlisle has failed to do, having allowed a fascinating collection of period shop fronts and narrow, cobbled lanes to be swept away to be replaced by an inner ring-road and a shopping development of characterless conventionality.

69

Chesterfield

What has happened in Carlisle could have been repeated in Chesterfield if the inhabitants had not rebelled against the destruction of their market place. Except for those few who go out of curiosity to see the famous Crooked Spire of St Mary and All Saints' Church, railway enthusiasts who make a pilgrimage to George Stephenson's tomb in Holy Trinity, and cricket lovers who make for one of the loveliest county grounds in England in Queen's Park, most visitors to Derbyshire head westward to the Peak and leave Chesterfield to its engineers and colliers. But the town is pleasanter than many other industrial centres and it is blessed with a particularly fine and spacious market place in which, not so long ago, wives were sold along with other useful commodities. In the early 1970s a development company, supported by the local council, proposed to 'restructure' the market place. The locals kicked, kicked hard, and went on kicking until the plan was shelved. There the matter rests. Chesterfield still has its market place intact, except for an ugly clutter of street furniture—road-signs and the like—that has grown up almost unnoticed over the last few years, and could now be suitably pruned. Another redevelopment plan may even now be in a state of gestation, but if so I expect its birth to be no easier than the last.

Berwick-upon-Tweed

I hope that our small towns will fight equally hard to resist unsuitable redevelopment plans, mostly forced upon them by traffic pressures, for these small market centres are among Britain's most precious jewels. Berwick-upon-Tweed and Conway are two of my favourites, both splendid walled towns. Berwick, indeed, must be the only town in England—and it is only just inside the border—where it is possible to make a complete town circuit on walls that, though much restored in the eighteenth century, had their origin in medieval times. For good measure, you can also walk on part of another wall erected in the reign of Elizabeth I. From these walls you get a fine view of the sea from one side and, from another side, of Berwick's three bridges spanning the Tweed: the low, stone, 15-arched bridge that was completed in 1634, its less handsome, concrete successor of 1928 that carries traffic on the Great North Road, and most striking of all, the lofty, 28-arched railway viaduct called the Royal Border Bridge over which the King's Cross–Edinburgh trains creep uneasily. But the best—and paradoxically the worst—view from the wall is over the red tiles of this busy little market town: best because of the unselfconscious charm of the tightly packed buildings; worst, partly because you can see what may happen to the town, partly because you can see what has already happened. What may happen is a widening of Northgate, which hardly anyone wants. What has already happened is that many of the buildings have gone to seed.

Berwick's problem is much the same as Edinburgh's. It has

too many good buildings and too little money. One in ten of its buildings is on the list of buildings to be preserved, the highest proportion of any town in Britain. One in five of its 12,000 inhabitants is retired. The cost of maintaining even its listed buildings would be an unbearable burden for a town of that size. To attempt it and let the other buildings go would be, as one inhabitant put it, 'like stuffing gold teeth into an elephant'.

A Preservation Trust has been launched, but it will take time to raise enough money to put the town to rights again. And time is not on Berwick's side, for some of the best buildings are empty and deteriorating daily. The transport planners may not be on Berwick's side either, as they seem to hanker after destructive road-widening rather than a by-pass that would solve at least one of the town's problems.

Conway

A by-pass is Conway's worry, too, but for rather different reasons. The town's position, with the castle dominating the Vale of Conway and the estuary that lapped against the town walls— the most complete in Britain—ideally suited Edward I's purpose, which was to keep the Welsh in order. Its narrow streets were an additional deterrent to an invading army taking the place by surprise, but they are wildly unsuitable for modern traffic. A dog crossing the road in front of two bicycles and a motor car is just about enough to cause a major traffic jam of the kind that Conway has lived with every summer since at least the 1930s. So a by-pass is wanted, but not in the form that has been proposed.

What is intended is a four-lane North Wales Expressway that will cross the estuary by a bridge at Conway, 50yd from the castle, and slice through the town and through the nearby coastal towns of Colwyn Bay, Llanfairfechan and Penmaenmawr. Apart from the scars that will be inflicted in the town itself, Conway objects strongly to the bridge, as it has three already and feels

25 Rail, road and foot bridges at Conway, North Wales. A proposal to build a fourth bridge is being strongly opposed

71

that a fourth will be a blot on the landscape. Of the three existing, Telford's road bridge is a handsome suspension bridge, replaced in 1958 by one more suited to modern traffic and now preserved as a national monument. Alongside is Robert Stephenson's railway bridge that outrageously tore straight through the town wall, but now seems to fit quite snugly into the landscape. But conservationists far beyond North Wales feel that the new road should be carried either well south of Conway or in a tunnel under the Conway river.

Petworth

Petworth in Sussex faces a similar dilemma. Petworth is a sort of Lilliputian town, not much bigger than a village, and as much dominated by its mansion, Petworth House, as Conway is by its castle; it is, as E. V. Lucas said, 'like Pompeii, with Vesuvius emitting glory far above'. Five busy main roads converge on the town's twisting main street that was inadequate even for the carriages, waggons and bicycles of Lucas's day seventy years ago. Today, timber-framed Tudor buildings tremble as cars and lorries grind by, almost scraping ancient walls. The need for a by-pass must have been obvious in coaching days and it has been a chief topic of conversation there for the last quarter of a century.

But as at Conway the problem has been to find a route that will not ruin the scenery, cost the earth or involve destruction of property. West Sussex County Council has consistently held

26 Seventeenth- and eighteenth-century houses at Petworth, Sussex

72

the view since 1951 that it should be driven through the 2,000-acre park that Capability Brown landscaped in the eighteenth century, this being the shortest, cheapest route and the least destructive of property. 'Sacrilege', says the National Trust which owns Petworth House and park, and Lord Egremont who lives as tenant in his ancestral home. But after much debate about alternative routes, it looks as if the council has won its case, and the road seems destined to cut through the park that Cobbett said 'nature formed here when she was in one of her most sportive moods', a mood captured in oils by Turner. If you want to see what Cobbett and Turner enjoyed, go soon to Petworth—the house, with its superb Grinling Gibbons carvings and fine pictures, and the park, with its rare herd of 400 deer, are open each summer. However carefully the new road is landscaped, the park can never be the same again. But in Petworth itself many people console themselves with the thought that the rape of the park will at least enable the town to retain its virtue. What strangers may ask is whether some other solution might not have been found to avoid violation of either park or town.

Burford

That same sort of problem, akin to the one that faced Isabella in *Measure for Measure*, now faces Burford in Oxfordshire. Like Petworth, it needs to lose some traffic; like Petworth, it doesn't know where to hide it. It is not the first time that Burford has had by-pass worries. It owes its Georgian prosperity to the opening of a regular coach route to London via Witney in 1761. Its fortunes and consequently its population declined after 1812 when an early 'by-pass'—now the A40—along the ridge above the southern edge of the town became the main route for coaches between Oxford and Cheltenham. Burford then went to sleep for more than a century, which is why it has hardly a building that is newer than the early nineteenth century and many a great deal older, even if some are disguised behind Georgian façades.

Now, the wheel—wheels perhaps would be more accurate—has turned full circle. Heavy lorries bound for Swindon from the Midlands and private cars full of tourists rumble up the High Street which I consider among the half-dozen most beautiful streets in all Britain, and from personal experience, one of the half-dozen least conducive to a good night's sleep. A by-pass seems essential and has been officially discussed for the last decade. But where should it run? All the answers seem to involve the desecration of the Windrush valley and its charming water-meadows.

But, as Isabella found, there is sometimes another choice besides death or dishonour. Both rape of the Windrush valley— a valley as delightful as the river name suggests—and the slow strangulation of Burford High Street could be avoided if a scheme of Duke Vincentio's ingenuity suggested by two local residents and eagerly supported by Michael Wright, in *Country*

Life (May 31, 1973), were taken up. Basically, the plan simply involves placing a weight restriction on the road through Burford and diverting heavy traffic onto the lightly used Fosse Way through Moreton-in-Marsh and Stow-on-the-Wold. It sounds simple. In practice, there may be more problems than meet the eye. But since there are few sights that meet the eye more beautiful than that of Burford rising up gently out of the Windrush valley, such problems could perhaps be overcome to achieve the sort of happy ending that Shakespeare achieved in *Measure for Measure*.

Tetbury

May there also be a happy ending for Tetbury's traffic problem. Tetbury lies over on the opposite side of the Cotswolds from Burford and seems to attract fewer tourists. The reason for this can only be that driving through it presents such an effort of concentration that there is no time to notice the beauty of its architecture. The slightly darker stone may not sparkle in the sunlight as those products of the Taynton quarries do at Burford; the buildings of Tetbury may look a little less carefully tended than those at Burford, and they stand too close to the pavements to leave room for such charming green sloping banks and bright front gardens as you see at the upper end of Burford's High Street.

Yet Tetbury is indisputably a highly attractive town. It has a fine seventeenth-century town hall built upon pillars, an early Gothic Revival church with box pews and a west gallery supported on wooden pillars, designed by Francis Hiorne in 1781; above all, it has Long Street, which is less well known than it deserves to be. It is, in the words of James Lees-Milne, 'a practically unbroken conglomeration of architectural monuments with lesser houses of the seventeenth, eighteenth and nineteenth century acting as a foil to them'. Some of the buildings may be a little tatty, like the one, formerly occupied by the Sir William Romney School, whose vandalised shell would have been demolished in 1974 but for ministerial intervention, but Long Street remains what some architectural experts then called 'the best street in the Cotswolds'.

Tetbury suffers from the usual troubles. Too many main roads converge outside the town; too many heavy lorries—460 of them on a single June day in 1974 when a census was taken—rattle through the narrow streets, shaking foundations and creating noise well above acceptable limits. As at Burford, some sort of weight restriction, rather than a by-pass, could be the best solution.

Bewdley and Ludlow

By-passes alone, it seems, can save those lovely riverside towns of Bewdley, on the Severn, and Ludlow, on the Severn's tributary, the Teme. This fact having been recognised in all the right places, both towns appeared assured of early relief until the public spending cuts of August 1976 put the by-pass schemes back into the waiting list.

Neither town can afford to wait long. Bewdley, as local opinion has it, is already 'crumbling under the strain of a tremendous number of heavy vehicles'. These vehicles, toing and froing between the Welsh Marches and the West Midlands, pour over Telford's river bridge from dawn to dusk and beyond. I can say this with experience, having once stood on Bewdley Bridge at dawn to find out if Leland's early-seventeenth century description, that 'att rising of the sunne the whole towne glittereth, being all of new building, as it were of gold' is still valid. It is not quite; it glows now rather than glitters because many of the timbered 'new buildings' were replaced or refaced in Queen Anne or Georgian red brick at a time when Bewdley was a booming river port. Most of those houses remain because the town fell asleep shortly afterwards when the new canal port of Stourport captured its trade, and has only been rudely reawakened in recent years by the din of motor traffic. Disregarding the noise, if you can, you will still find Bewdley beautiful 'att rising of the sunne' or at any other time.

That goes for Ludlow, also. Its castle, where Milton's *Comus* was first performed in 1634, towers magnificently above the river. It has a wealth of timbered buildings, including the superb Feathers inn. You find it hard to dispute Edmund Vale's opinion that 'it is the most complete medieval town in England'. You find it equally hard to tolerate the traffic that flows through it 'like a continual goods train'.

Cuts must be accepted in times of economic stress. But cuts can develop into festering wounds. Bewdley and Ludlow both need attention, urgently.

Holt

Across the country in East Anglia, Holt is destined to have a by-pass, though the chosen route is not to everyone's taste. Though the remedy may not be pleasant, it will be better than the disease, which is, again, trafficitis, caused not so much by heavy lorries as by holiday traffic oozing through the zig-zag main street on its way to Sheringham, Cromer and Great Yarmouth. As at Tetbury, the strange thing is that so few motorists stop to explore Holt. Maybe it lacks any noted individual building. One tends to notice only such oddities as an eighteenth-century obelisk that gives the mileage to innumerable places around, and a church clock with but one hand. However, the whole town wears an air of quiet distinction that tells of Georgian prosperity, though the haphazard arrangement of shops round the market place suggests an earlier origin as market stalls. Holt is one of those clean, fresh-looking Norfolk market towns that add so much distinction to that pleasant county, and it is all the better for being refurbished a decade or so ago in a Civic Trust pilot scheme.

I might have reversed my usual advice and warned people

27 Much street furniture, like this old horse trough, is swiftly disappearing

to wait to see Holt until the by-pass is built, but on second thoughts it might be as well to go now in case a new road mars the quietly attractive surrounding countryside, and because three other towns in East Anglia need to be seen soon before it is too late.

Sudbury

One is Sudbury in Suffolk, the 'Eatanswell' of Dickens's *Pickwick Papers* and the birthplace of Thomas Gainsborough, whose old home is preserved as a memorial and local arts centre. But there is more in this thriving little town that needs to be preserved. Careless redevelopment is robbing Sudbury of some of the character that must have helped to inspire Gainsborough to paint. A row of weavers' cottages, a reminder of Sudbury's former importance in the cloth industry, has recently been demolished to make way, possibly, for a car-park. A sports complex is to be built obtrusively in the Stour water-meadows without any thought of landscaping the scenery. A scene that Constable—born a few miles downstream—might well have painted is to be thoughtlessly destroyed. A sports complex sounds an excellent idea, but where and how it is placed needs more careful thought if Sudbury is to retain at least some of its distinctive character.

Huntingdon

The second East Anglian town I have in mind is Huntingdon, and here again a water-meadow looms large. Indeed, this is a

76

very large water-meadow, extending over 360 acres, which makes it one of the biggest in Britain. It is called Portholme, was 'common to the freeholders and tenants of the Manor of Huntingdon' as far back as 1205, and was described by Camden as 'the largest and most flowery spot the sun ever beheld' which is flowery enough in itself. Camden was right in calling it flowery. Portholme is scheduled a Site of Special Scientific Interest because its herb-rich sward supports some rare plant species. The snake's head fritillary, for instance, grows nowhere else in the old county of Huntingdonshire, and the narrow leaved drop-wort, that grows exclusively in water-meadows, is only slightly less rare.

The meadow is now endangered because its present owners, the London Anglers' Association, intend to allow the gravel beneath the sward to be worked and to use some of the income to develop a series of 25-acre fisheries, a picnic area and a nature area. To judge from the Association's excellent past record, these sites will be well managed and provide pleasure. But however carefully safeguarded Portholme is, its original form will be lost for ever. If the local council, which has not got overmuch beauty in Huntingdon to safeguard, had stepped in and bought the water-meadow when it was up for sale in 1962, another piece of our national heritage might have been out of danger.

Cambridge

Sixteen miles south-eastward, Cambridge is the third East Anglian town which could run into trouble. Here again, the potential menace is not at its superb heart—though some odd development is going on in Petty Cury—but in Grantchester Meadows, across which a final link may be built in what is ironically called the outer ring relief road for Cambridge. It could, if it is ever built, relieve the town of some of its traffic, but it will most certainly bring no relief to the hearts and minds of those townsfolk and dons who wrote indignantly to *The Times* in the closing weeks of 1975. Grantchester Meadows are as dear to Cambridge hearts as Christ Church Meadows to Oxford hearts. It is the nearest accessible area of riverscape to the centre of Cambridge, a place of great natural beauty providing the ideal approach to Rupert Brooke's village, and a popular resort for 'amorous undergraduates and dons walking off their considerable Sunday lunches'. There is no likelihood of the road's being built just yet, but many people, not by any means all from either Cambridge or Grantchester, would be much happier if the full-stop in this sentence could follow 'built'.

6 Vanishing Villages

The by-pass, a curse and a blessing

The people of Grantchester are no doubt just as concerned about a possible encroachment by a new road on what, in name anyway, are their meadows as are the citizens of Cambridge—only there are fewer of them to make a fuss. Because the majority of Britons live in towns, and because the phrase has a pleasantly alliterative ring, we have given much thought in recent years to the problem of traffic in towns and not quite enough to the almost equally worrying problem of too many vehicles in villages. This is not quite the case for the inhabitants of places like Tarvin and Tarporley, who have been trying to live with gradually worsening traffic problems for many years.

Tarvin and Tarporley may sound like a couple of old-time music hall comedians but in fact they are very real, very attractive Cheshire villages five miles apart and stretched out along the line of the Roman Watling Street, now the A51, both at points where other busy roads come in. Their residents are asking loudly and clearly for by-passes to be built quickly, and none, I should imagine, more anxiously than the occupants of two pleasant Georgian houses at a sharp bend in the road at Tarvin. They have the unnerving experience, many hundred times a day, of seeing juggernauts steering straight for their front windows before swerving violently away almost at the point of impact, which must be rather like being at the receiving end of one of those traditional circus knife-throwing acts. Winding my way sinuously through Kelsall, which is the next village to Tarvin on the A34, and a little later the same day passing through the handsome mill village of Upper Tean on the A50 in Staffordshire, it struck me that here were two more villages where by-passes would not come amiss.

Nor would it at Avebury in Wiltshire, which lies on the A361 close to its junction with the A4. It also lies inside a prehistoric stone circle that must have been erected for some ceremonial purpose. The A361 cuts almost sacreligiously right through the circle, which is rather like running a road through the nave of some great cathedral. The spirit of the past is so strong in Avebury that even the traffic cannot quite ruin it, but if the traffic could be channelled onto a by-pass the atmosphere of the

78

village would certainly be enhanced and risk of injuries to visitors greatly reduced.

To see just what benefits a by-pass can confer on a village, you need to go to places like Bridge in Kent or Ombersley in Worcestershire. Bridge, just south-east of Canterbury, consists mainly of a long, straight, narrow main street approached on the Dover side by a steep hill and a narrow bridge. All these lay until recently on the A2, the main London–Dover road that follows the line of the Roman Watling Street in an impeccably straight line that invited speed. The invitation was all too often accepted. Lorries sometimes ran out of control on the hill and ended up by making a mess of some house or other in the village. Bridge had been promised the by-pass it so obviously needed, but it was kept waiting like an anxious bride-to-be for the happy day while the nerves of its inhabitants and the walls of its buildings continued to be frayed until a by-pass was eventually opened in the summer of 1976. Ombersley is another attractive village that was almost ruined by traffic. When I first went there a few years ago, I could hardly cross the road to look at the many picturesque black and white half-timbered houses, with a splendid Dower House sitting almost on top of a road island at the busiest spot in the village. But all that has changed, I discovered on a recent visit. The long-promised by-pass has now been built, peace has been restored, and you can admire the houses in comparative comfort.

Yet what is good for Bridge and Ombersley is not necessarily good for every village. There are villages whose inhabitants understandably feel themselves threatened by proposed by-passes or motorways. Several of these lie on, or close to, the line of the proposed M54 in east Shropshire. One is Tong, which has only recently cleared most of its traffic out of its main street by way of an A41 by-pass, restoring the right sort of atmosphere for the enjoyment of its fine church. Now, it seems, the traffic is to come back on the A54, and you wonder how all those long-dead Vernons, whose splendid tombs enrich the church, would react to this situation.

Perhaps they would protest as vigorously as the people of the tiny black and white magpie-style Cheshire village of Barthomley (with its Norman church and thatched pub of 1614), who sent a deputation to Westminster to object to a proposed M6 link road bisecting their parish. They might, you feel, even cause the Great Bell in the noble tower of Tong Church to be rung, an event reserved, according to a seventeenth-century notice in the church porch, for particularly momentous occasions.

Neither Tong nor Barthomley is likely to vanish if the by-passes come, but much of their charm will. They would be bound to suffer changes in character, inevitably for the worse. The building of such roads brings not only additional traffic, with its attendant dangers, noise and litter but also opens up new areas for commuters to settle in, so bringing the town out into the country.

Suburban subtopia

The desire to escape from the city workshop to the peace of the countryside at the end of the day is natural and understandable. It goes back a long way in history. Arthur Young foresaw in 1789 the dramatic changes that the opening of the London–Horsham turnpike road was likely to bring to the villages of the Sussex Weald, that 'very pretty country' of 'stiff land, small fields, broad hedgerows, . . . invariably thickly planted with fine-growing oak trees', as Cobbett called it. The turnpike brought the Weald 'within a short morning's drive of London', and thus attracted the first generation of wealthy commuters. The coming of the railways hastened the process. Dormitory towns, like Haywards Heath and Burgess Hill sprang up on former common land, and a thin line of villas began to creep across the Weald. The motor car increased the tempo, and plans are now accepted for a corridor of residential and industrial development across the Weald between Crawley and the South Downs. It is pointless to grumble at planners who are simply recognising an historical pattern laid down when the London–Horsham turnpike opened in 1756. But soon it may no longer be true to write, as Peter Brandon did in *The Sussex Landscape* in 1973, that 'a distant view across the Weald conveys the impression that almost all the Sussex Weald is still unbroken woodland as was the Saxon *Andredesweald*.' It seems that those early commuters failed to disentangle themselves from the city, and merely dragged it out with them.

If no other city spreads itself quite so widely as London, a government report issued as recently as April 1976 confirms that 'commuter hinterlands' throughout Britain are still spreading. Most villages within, say, ten miles of large urban centres are now disguised in featureless suburban trappings. There are a few notable exceptions of course. Dulwich is still recognisably a village inside London. Strelley is still an entirely unspoilt and seemingly remote village on the outskirts of Nottingham, if you turn your back on the vast Bilborough housing estate, and there are still leafy roads and a large area of private parkland at Norton within the city of Sheffield. Darley Abbey, inside the borough of Derby, is still essentially—despite some modern suburban intrusions—a well preserved eighteenth-century cotton-mill village, with just one, poorly preserved, fragment of its Augustinian abbey standing to explain the village name. But though that last remnant of the Abbey may soon disintegrate, the industrial village should survive intact because the local authority acted promptly in making it a conservation area.

That sort of urgency might have saved more of Shardlow, some ten miles farther south. But Shardlow's conservation area covers too little and came too late (1975) to preserve intact a unique inland canal port. A few warehouses have gone; so have the handsome stables for the towing-horses; a canalside tavern has become a private house. Subtopia has put its clammy fingers

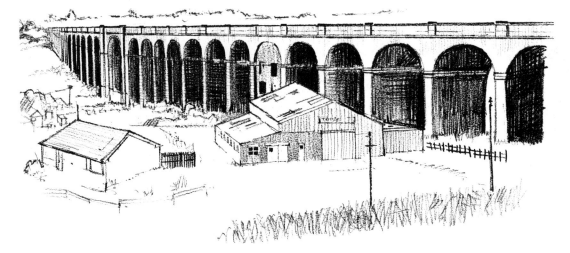

on the village, but has not yet choked the life out of it. Shardlow is still Britain's most complete inland village port.

Modern Shardlow is a long village straggling on either side of the A6 road. Originally it was two separate settlements: a small agricultural village half a mile north of the Trent, and an equally small river port called Wilden Ferry (later Cavendish Bridge) at the water's edge. Then in the 1770s, James Brindley cut his Trent and Mersey Canal—at that time the most ambitious civil engineering exercise in Britain since the Romans built their roads—linking east and west coasts. At Shardlow, less than a mile from the eastern terminus, an inland canal port sprang up, filling the gap between the two earlier settlements, and enough of it survives to explain why early nineteenth-century writers called it 'little Liverpool', especially now that the growth of pleasure boating has brought renewed life to its wharves.

Life, a life of their own, is what so many of these new suburbs so often lack. This may sound paradoxical. Surely, all these new houses have brought new life to old villages, you may think. But all too often they have brought only new lives, not new life. Most of the new houses are likely to be occupied by people who have their roots in the town, people who earn their money in town by day and spend it there on entertainment in the evening. Their suburban villages are just dormitories—bedroom, breakfast-bar and garages the only essential components of their houses. And the houses themselves often look mass-produced by townsmen for townsmen, with little regard for local variation.

You can see this sort of unfortunate development taking place in what is sometimes called High Norfolk, south-west of Norwich, where the land reaches what is by East Anglian standards an almost breath-taking 200ft. In an attractive stretch of countryside in which, ironically, the council housing has been rightly praised, several once-pleasing villages—with Poringland a particularly glaring example—are being swamped by subtopian private houses that seem utterly out of context in what was a purely rural scene.

28 Many monuments to the great age of the railways, like this viaduct, are being allowed to decay

Villages abandoned

The sort of insensitive development described is inexcusable, but there is a defence that can be offered against my charge against turning once-rural villages into suburbia. 'If we hadn't allowed this development,' I can hear local councillors saying, 'these villages would have died.' They could have a valid point. Villages have died in the past, as I discovered to my embarrassment some years ago when I was casually trying to locate a Derbyshire village called Barton Blount that I had seen mentioned in documents but had never visited. 'Barton Blount,' echoed a passing walker whom I stopped to seek directions. 'I'm afraid you're about three hundred years too late. But it lies somewhere under that field.' He waved an arm in the general direction of a large humpy field where sheep were grazing on close-cropped grass.

Such was my awakening to the fact that villages can vanish for reasons that have nothing to do with the restless sea. Since then, books by Maurice Beresford, W. G. Hoskins and others have taught me that possibly hundreds of inland villages, many of them from the grasslands of the eastern Midlands, have gone from the face of the earth. At ground level it is difficult for the layman to recognise an abandoned village site unless, as at Calceby in Lincolnshire and Martinthorpe in what used to be Rutland, the ruins of a church survive. But from the air it is easy enough to see that a sunken track across a field was once a village street and to trace the fossilised outlines of a flanking cottages.

Why did these places vanish? The sheep bleat back the answer, along with the wind sighing through the grass making the only sounds that disturb the serenity of Barton Blount. They drove out the labourers from their cottages five hundred years or so ago, being more profitable than crops in days when the wool trade accounted for three quarters of England's exports. The wages of one shepherd were easier to find than the wages of a dozen labourers to reap and sow, especially when the land was as impoverished as at significantly named Hungry Bentley, another lost village a mile or two across empty fields from Barton Blount.

It is easy to say that all this happened way back in history and that history does not repeat itself. Easy, but not entirely convincing. Maps still mark a village with the unlikely name of Snap just below the ancient Ridgeway in Wiltshire, but the village itself died as late as the nineteenth century and there is precious little left now above ground. Bessingham in north Norfolk was dying on its feet when I was last there in the early 1970s. Its manor house was empty, its pub shut and vandalised, more than half the cottages tenantless and decaying. Its population had fallen from 150 to less than 40 under a succession of squires who refused to relet the cottages as they became vacant. The village was up for sale when I was there, but the remaining inhabitants were not optimistic that a change of ownership would save the place, and I left feeling that even subtopian torpor would be preferable to this steady bleeding to death. But Bessingham is a good 20 miles from Norwich, five from the nearest main road, which in a thinly populated county poorly served by public transport puts it outside commuterland.

There may be exceptional circumstances at Bessingham to account for the speed of its decline, as there must be to explain why the once lovely Cotswold village of Great Barrington is similarly dying on its foundations. Rhulen, in what used to be Radnorshire and is now Powys, is more typical of the slow decay that is gradually eroding the more remote agricultural villages. It is an attractive little place in the valley of the Edw, but very much off the beaten track since the drovers stopped beating their tracks over Rhulen Hill towards Hereford. Once it had a fulling mill and a corn mill to give alternative employment to the staple agricultural industry, and two inns to provide refreshment. Today, the mills and the inns have gone, like the school and even the chapel. The primitive little church, with whitewashed rubble-stone walls and a timber bellcote, is the sole surviving communal building, but it has had no incumbent since 1974. The population has dwindled by more than 75 per cent since 1847 to a mere 30 or so. The unwanted houses have become outbuildings or have disappeared altogether, their stones having been put to use on neighbouring farms. Rhulen lies at the end of a valley road that makes no more than a token gesture towards climbing the green hill beyond. Sadly, it looks as if figuratively, too, the village is coming to the end of the road, though with a good deal more dignity than Bessingham or Great Barrington can muster.

There is a feeling of remoteness about Rhulen, but in fact it is only ten miles from Builth Wells and not much more than that from Llandrindod Wells. However, neither of these is a town that one would want to escape from and there is no large population centre anywhere within commuting distance of even the most road-happy motorist, while public transport is nonexistent. This absence of public transport is one of the main causes of the decline of these more remote villages.

The root cause, though, is much the same as the one that killed Barton Blount, Martinthorpe and other now deserted places so long ago; an agricultural revolution. Modern mechanised farming requires little labour. The old purely agricultural village, like Flora Thompson's Lark Rise, in which every man and boy except the vicar and the doctor worked on the land within a mile or two of his home, is an historical memory. The sons of the farmworkers of the pre-combine age now commute to work in the nearest town 'in Anglias or on mopeds', like the young men of Ronald Blythe's Akenfield. Or they do until a new, town-bred wife or the rising cost of petrol compels them to find an urban home. Their children are sent to a town school, and the village primary and infants' school eventually closes because the numbers have dropped into the thirties or less. Then the few remaining young marrieds move out of the village in search of a handy school, and only the older people are left.

This is the story in many of our old farming villages beyond the commuter fringe. It is certainly the tale of most villages in the central and south-western areas of the Peak District; of Sheen, for example, in the Staffordshire section of the Peak Park, which had shed rather more than a quarter of its population in the forty years before 1971. It does not happen on the east side of the Peak, where the villages are less than half an hour's drive from Sheffield and are, by way of a bonus, better served by public transport. Those villages are growing, but the new houses and the old agricultural cottages that became vacant are snapped up by Sheffield commuters with money to spare, so that places like Hathersage, Baslow, Froggatt and Ashford-in-the-Water are gradually becoming single-class commuter villages, a phenomenon that the Peak Park Joint Planning Board has recognised with some distaste and is now trying to discourage.

Second home settlements

Even the commuter village is usually preferable to the 'second home' village where most of the houses are shut up for much of the year because the local people have been outbid on the property market by wealthy townsfolk seeking holiday homes. There are villages in the Cotswolds and other beautiful areas of Britain where the locals have been banished to council houses on the fringe, to live like Red Indians in the reservations, while their old cottages are inhabited only at weekends in summer and during school holidays. I have been told that there are villages completely deserted during the winter, but I have never succeeded in finding one. What I have found on the Devon and Cornish coasts, where there are around 7,000 second homes, are villages where at least a quarter of the houses are shut up from October to March. Much the same state of winter hibernation afflicts many villages in the old county of Caernarvon, where nearly 3,000 houses are merely holiday homes, and on the coasts of Dorset and Hampshire.

Brook in the Isle of Wight is typical of many of these second home villages, and I mention it simply because I had a sort of vague, nodding acquaintance with it for several years during the war when it was one of the first places we could see from the sea as we approached the Needles entrance to the Solent from the south west. Gazing at it longingly through binoculars, I thought it would be pleasant to live there, perched up a hundred feet or so above Brook Bay. J. B. Priestley evidently had the same idea and did live there for several years. Unfortunately, a high proportion of the houses in what I have seen lately described, perhaps a bit unfairly, as 'a desolate place' are now owned by people who do not live there—for much of the year, anyway—and an element of desolation is creeping in.

The supreme example, though, of this sort of absentee ownership must be those picture-postcard villages of Robin Hood's

Bay, Runswick Bay and Staithes on the Yorkshire coast. One would be hard put to it to think of three more picturesque coastal villages so close together anywhere else in Britain. All three cling precariously to steep cliff sides; precariously in a double sense at Robin Hood's Bay, the 'Bramblewick' of Leo Walmsley's delightful novels, for the sea has been eating away at the cliff for centuries, as the boulder-strewn beach testifies (illustration 29).

The three villages conform to a common pattern forced on them by the lie of the land. The fishermen's cottages squat just above the shore, or line the steep, narrow main street behind, where one family's side window overlooks their neighbours' chimney pots. Above, on the cliff top, are the newer, larger houses of retired sea captains and prosperous 'incomers'. That was how Leo Walmsley saw these places. But since the war the social pattern has changed somewhat. The fishermen's cottages have been bought at inflated prices by business and professional people from the Yorkshire woollen towns who use them as holiday cottages, while the fishermen have either sunk their new capital to buy themselves houses at the back of the village or moved into council houses that have sprung up 'on top o't' bank'.

29 Going: houses at Robin Hood's Bay, Yorkshire, precariously perched above a beach strewn with boulders from cliff falls

30 Blakeney, Norfolk, a splendid
example of local preservation

'There's only two of these cottages occupied in t'winter,' I
was told by an old man in a harbourside house at Staithes.
'There's me and an old widow lady, and we're both turned
eighty.' In bad weather their groceries were lowered down the
cliff side in a basket at the end of a rope.

At Robin Hood's Bay, the position is much the same. Few
friendly lights shine reassuringly seaward from 'bottom o't'
bank.' At Runswick, there is a slight variation. The cottages,
more widely spaced, have been enlarged and modernised; many
seem to be permanently occupied. This 'tarting-up' has been
generally well done, so that a newcomer to the Bay will still be
struck by its charm. But remembering the genuine, unselfconscious beauty of the cottages as they were before World War
II, I find them now slightly phoney and belonging to the world
of the glossy magazine. Outwardly, these villages are still lovely
and unspoilt—despite that potash mine just behind Staithes—
and certainly should be visited, but if you know them well
already you may feel that they have lost something; their main
reason for existence perhaps. The body has been well preserved:
the soul, it seems to me, has gone.

Farther down the east coast, where a lonely, evocative mile of
marshland separates the lovely flint and pantile villages from the
sea, Blakeney (illustration 30) and its neighbour Wiveton have
miraculously preserved both body and soul. The flint-built
cottages, mostly 200 or 300 years old and often huddled together
round small courtyards for protection against the biting North
Sea gales, have been renovated and modernised but are still
mainly occupied by local people. What happened here was that

an exceptionally able and determined lady called Mrs Norah Clogstoun read the game remarkably accurately, stepped in almost before the first potential second homers in Nottingham and Leicester had pointed their cars towards the Norfolk coast, and formed with some like-minded friends a body called the Blakeney Neighbourhood Society, of which she became the first chairman. That was in 1946, when fishermen's cottages, deteriorating after six years of enforced neglect during the war, could be bought for the sort of price that would not buy a decent washing machine today. By 1950 the housing society had bought thirty cottages in Blakeney and Wiveton at an average price of £106 each. It then moved the families into temporary accommodation, repaired and improved the houses, at an average cost of £115 each, which included the installation of electricity, and finally moved the families back again, raising their rents by one shilling a week, despite howls of protest.

With hindsight, we can see that this sort of scheme should have been carried out nationwide. A few similar societies did spring up and even formed a National Federation of Housing Societies. Some, like the Gwynedd Housing Association in North Wales still do useful work in an area where one third of the houses, including one new house in every three, are second homes, in buying houses and renting them at low rents to needy families. But overall, what was lacking was people with the foresight and drive of Mrs Clogstoun.

Of course there is a case for the second homers, the well heeled commuters and retired people who buy and do up property in the most attractive parts of Britain. They not only perform valuable rescue jobs on old property but are often much more zealous than the natives in fighting to resist any unharmonious development around their new territory. I remember grousing aloud over the air about the tarting-up of lovely old cottages in Constable's Stour Valley. 'Don't forget,' replied a friend who was one of the tarters, 'if we hadn't done this, the cottage would have been demolished.' He was right in his particular case, and there are many similar examples.

Rhyd, high up in Snowdonia, is one. Basically, it was a quarrying village. When the quarries closed, the inhabitants gradually moved out in search of other work. When only two or three families remained, and the village seemed to be dying, newcomers began to arrive. Mostly they were people seeking a second home for weekends and holidays, attracted by Rhyd's lovely setting, almost within sight of the sea. These same attractions also brought a few retired people and at least one family hoping to make a living by making Welsh love-spoons and similar items for the tourist trade. About half the houses are shut up in winter, which does not make for an ideal community, but at least this attractive village has been saved from total dereliction, which was the fate of Nant Gwrtheyrn.

This was a village to which death came suddenly. Its rotting remains can be found, not too easily, on the north coast of the

Lleyn Peninsula in what Thomas Pennant in the eighteenth century called a 'gloomy hollow'. To reach it, you take an unsignposted lane uphill towards the coast from Llanaelhaern and drive for about a mile until the lane peters out. After that, you walk down a rough, steep, twisting track into a bowl of breathtaking splendour. And there, clinging to the nearest possible approximation to level ground, are the shells of 27 terraced cottages, a couple of farmhouses, a school and the inevitable chapel, now roofless and forlorn. Beyond, on the beach, are the rusting machinery and rickety landing-stage that served, until 1963, a thriving granite quarry.

That first sight of the village is a moment of high drama. You know at once just how those sailors felt who found the *Marie Celeste* deserted under full sail. Here is a working village that suddenly ceased to work; a modern Pompeii engulfed by the eruption of an economic volcano.

The prosaic fact is that concrete replaced granite in the making of paving slabs for town streets, and the quarry shut down. The buildings could never be mentioned in the same breath as those of Pompeii, but the setting is superb, despite Pennant's gloom. And the wonder is not so much that the village was abandoned but that it was ever built at all in that land-locked bay to which provisions and fuel could surely only have come by sea.

New life from industry

Nant Gwrtheyrn is well worth a visit soon, while the remnants of the village remain, for those fit enough to face the lung-breaking climb back. And while you are in the area, it is worth looking at Llanaelhaern, which has received a good deal of publicity in recent years as a near moribund village which is being revived. Crafts and light industries are being coaxed into the village by enthusiastic inhabitants, led by an energetic young doctor from Liverpool, expressly to give the village the kiss-of-life.

This sort of treatment is probably right for those decaying agricultural villages that I have mentioned. There is no intrinsic reason why light industry, as distinct from the heavy and extractive industries, need be ugly. The founders of the Industrial Revolution in the cotton industry put up most felicitous buildings in what were virtually company villages, like Styal, Cheshire, and Cromford, Derbyshire. Styal is now owned by the National Trust, which has modernised the workers' cottages without altering the village layout, and Sir Richard Arkwright's Cromford, which has survived almost intact from the late eighteenth century, is now safely protected within a conservation area, as is Jedidiah Strutt's Milford, a few miles south along the narrow Derwent Valley, where the houses cling to steep terraces above the river.

Modern industry can do equally well when it tries. A decidedly sizable industrial complex at Rocester in Staffordshire, traditionally a mixed agricultural and textile community, has been so carefully landscaped in a hollow in almost parklike surroundings that it is virtually invisible until you are a stone's throw away. At Kilburn, in the Hambleton Hills of North Yorkshire under the shadow of the White Horse of Roulston Scar that was carved out on the hillside by a schoolmaster and his pupils in 1857, the workshops where Robert Thompson produced his famous hand-made oak furniture, and signed them with his tiny carved mouse trade-mark, are now run by his grandsons and some 30 other craftsmen, providing the major source of employment in this handsome village of stone-built houses without detracting anything from its charm.

Kilburn points the way that the village of the future should ideally go, but few villages can rear their own native geniuses, like Robert Thompson, son of the local joiner, who was born there in 1876, and industry brought in from outside tends to be heavy handed and to change the character of a village too drastically. This is happening at Paddock Wood in Kent, which is rapidly dropping all pretence of being a village in its new role as the capital of the hop country. While architecturally and historically, little has been lost here, for Paddock Wood was a product of the railway age with few old buildings, there is a danger that the increased traffic and industrial development may change the character of the more beautiful surrounding villages.

It follows then that the planners need to watch most carefully the types of industry that come to the villages and the effect

31 Breedon-on-the-hill, Leicestershire

89

they are likely to have on the whole area around. What is not usually welcomed, as the villagers of East Grimstead in Wiltshire can testify, is something like quarrying, which inevitably brings noise and dirt.

East Grimstead, just south-east of Salisbury, is too small and off the beaten track to be a tourist attraction, but it sits comfortably, and until 1967, peacefully, in what a Department of the Environment inspector called 'a very beautiful part of the rural Wiltshire countryside'. What disturbed its peace in 1967 was the establishment of a chalk quarry on eleven acres of land just outside the village. Equally disturbing to conservationists everywhere was the way part of the 'public' inquiry was held in private, the excuse given being the highly confidential technical evidence about the processes involved in dealing with the uniquely white East Grimstead chalk. Permission to work the site was granted for five years, but an extension of both the quarry and time limit was later given by the Secretary of State against the advice of his inspector, who had in fact denied the uniqueness of East Grimstead chalk. So an attractive rural village is to be hidden under a haze of chalk dust for another decade or so, and scathing remarks about 'talk and chalk' are not confined to educational circles in that part of Wiltshire.

Obviously, this is the wrong sort of treatment for East Grimstead. In the short term it may provide a few extra jobs for the local men; in the longer term nothing but a large, ugly hole in the ground. Only urgent 'national interest' should excuse this sort of desecration.

But just what sort of inroads one allows industry to make into our villages without ruining them is not always as easy to decide as it seems to have been at East Grimstead, where the answer should surely have been 'not an inch'. Breedon on the Hill (illustration 31) in Leicester presents a more difficult case. It is a pleasant village, where, as so often in the East Midlands, a fairly harmonious balance seems to have been struck between agriculture and industry—limestone quarrying. The quarry owners, local people, are the chief employers and main benefactors of the village which, regardless of its name, clings quite felicitously to the foot and lower slopes of the hill. Only the church is literally on the hill, 180ft above the village, on a site that has been used for Christian worship for 1,200 years. The church on the hill is a landmark that can be seen for miles around across the valley of the Trent. And for those with the energy to climb up, or the nerve to take their cars up the steep, twisting but smooth-surfaced track, the church is most rewarding, containing fragments of remarkable Saxon sculpture arranged in friezes round the interior walls. Mainly of eighth century date, and depicting human figures as well as fabulous birds and beasts, they were discovered in a buttress early in this century and presumably belonged to the original Saxon monastery. They are, I believe, unique in England, and certainly ought to be seen, as should the elaborate Shirley family pew of 1627—'a large and strange seat', as a contemporary writer put it—the family tombs, and the Swithland slate headstones in the churchyard. Unfortunately, the hill itself is being eaten away by quarrying. Most of the Iron Age ramparts that encircled the summit have gone. Great chunks of raw, reddish rock now glare out across the valley from what was once a grassy hillside.

What should be done? Stop the quarrying at once, at least on that side of the hill? That is the answer that springs immediately to mind. But this would cause much unemployment and hardship; ruin village life in what seems to be a happy, flourishing community.

Changing with the times

Depriving a village of its main source of employment in order to preserve its pretty face is like extracting all the juice from an orange. It looks all right outwardly for a time, but eventually it withers and dies. There are places where such action might be justified; Breedon is probably not one of them. Better there to let quarrying continue, so long as there is no direct threat to the church. If there were, more drastic action would be needed, because Breedon church is far too rich a jewel to be tarnished.

Conservationists and planners need, then, to take each case on its merits. No village should be abandoned while people still want to go on living there. There may have seemed excellent reasons for moving the remaining inhabitants out of Skinningrove in North Yorkshire and demolishing the houses when the steel works closed. Architecturally, the village spoilt what before the nineteenth century must have been a lovely setting. It was—and is—an ugly blot on a delightful coastline. Yet many of its inhabitants wanted to stay where their roots were and, so far, they have been allowed to do so, as have the people of several former colliery villages in County Durham, who were also scheduled by the planners for 'dispersal'. All these villages started out as artificial creations built to serve the needs of nine-teenth-century industrialists. Now that no such need exists, it may have seemed sensible to the planners to move the people, demolish the houses and tidy up the sites. But what the planners overlooked—at Skinningrove and in Durham—was the community spirit that had grown up in those places. Not even to restore beauty—and certainly not for administrative tidiness—should it be permissible to destroy a community.

Nor is it possible to preserve a community completely unchanged. This may seem to contradict what I have said previously, but this is not the case. The planners should aim to preserve the essential character of a place and every good building that it has, not to create an artificial fossil that pretends that the twentieth century has not happened. Lavenham in Suffolk, for instance—although a town rather than a village—is essentially medieval and Tudor *in character*. It is an almost miraculous survival. But it also has a few later buildings, almost all good of their kind, that do not detract from that character. So it is with

32 Cavendish, Suffolk, a still unspoilt village

such villages as Cavendish (illustration 32) and Kersey, Castle Combe and Colston Basset, Northleach and Thornton-le-Dale and many more. They have retained their dignity and character, neither obsessed with the past nor allowing themselves to be carried away by the present.

Those two dangers, and a sensible compromise, seem to me to be exemplified by three Cotswold villages: Lower Slaughter, Bourton-on-the-Water and Guiting Power. Lower Slaughter is a charming show-place that must be one of Britain's most beautiful villages. Lots of visitors come to admire it, as I have done several times. If I lived there, I should want to keep it just as it is, which is undoubtedly what its inhabitants strive to do. But I just wonder if they may strive a bit too hard. Is it perhaps too good to be true? You feel you want to wipe your shoes before entering the village, and when you have left you wonder if the villagers have been out to clean up any dust you may have caused. You feel there the slight sense of constraint that you have in the home of some over-house-proud housewife, like Dylan Thomas's Mrs Ogmore-Pritchard.

Go on to Bourton-on-the-Water (illustration 33), the next village southward across the Fosse Way, and you see that Lower Slaughter is, excusably, simply over-compensating. Bourton has, as a Victorian might have said, sold its soul to the devil of commercialism. In the old tradition of the courtesan, Bourton has discovered that her face is her fortune and has proceeded to turn her assets into hard cash. There has been no shortage of

92

clients. On Easter Sunday 1975, snow was lying on the top of the Cotswolds, it was snowing hard in Stow-on-the-Wold, where the wind proverbially blows cold, but in Bourton any snow on the ground had been trodden into slush by the crowds. I drove through at a walking pace in a long line of cars competing for non-existent parking space. There was no chance to take in the beauty of those honey-coloured stone houses, of the lovely Windrush flowing under the bridges. I stopped looking for room to park and headed for the open wold where the roads were empty, the snow clean and the air keen. A decade ago, Bourton-on-the-Water was another of Britain's loveliest villages. Since then, its appearance has not changed; its atmosphere has. On a weekday in winter, it is still lovely, but in the spring its fancies lightly change to thoughts of exploitation, and it should be avoided until late autumn.

Guiting Power, on the other hand, need not be avoided at any time. It is a friendly, welcoming sort of place, not so well known as Bourton or Lower Slaughter, which lie just to the south, but wearing almost equally handsomely its suit of Cotswold stone. It is also very much a living village, but without any hint of Bourton's commercialism. Changes are taking place there because the landowner is gradually transferring his estate to a charitable trust, the Guiting Manor Trust, to prevent it being broken up by taxation and inflation. Restorations and modernisations are being subtly carried out, farm buildings are being converted into flatlets for old people and young couples, with

33 In danger from commercialism, Bourton-on-the-Water, Gloucestershire

93

priorities to village people or their connections. You have the feeling that Guiting Power is a good place to live in; that it has preserved its tradition and charm and is carrying them on into the twenty-first century.

We need lots of Guiting Powers, combining the best of the past with the improved amenities of the present. And we need to preserve those small, almost insignificant features of our villages that help to give them their individual character: buildings and bits of street furniture which are hardly noticed until one realises with regret that they have gone. I am thinking of things like village lock-ups, like those at Breedon, and just over the Derbyshire border at Ticknall and Smisby and one farther north at Alfreton that some councillors believe should be demolished. Another, at Lingfield, one of Surrey's prettiest villages, is almost obscured now by modern buildings, and slowly decaying unnoticed. It could be that Lingfield people are already doing something to save it. If not they should do so at once, just as the villagers of Crich in Derbyshire should ensure the safety of their large fourfold horse trough, designed possibly to slake the thirst of packhorse teams carrying lead across the Derbyshire hills. Items like these, and the crumbling eighteenth-century 'bee wall' at Hemingfield, near Barnsley, with its 36 rectangular recesses, or boles, each used for giving warmth and shelter to a straw hive, are slices of living history we can ill afford to lose.

7 Buildings in Danger

Crumbling churches

On a May morning in 1975 the tall, west tower of St Mary Magdalene, Bildeston in Suffolk collapsed. Nobody was hurt. The builders working on the tower had a minute's notice that something was wrong, just enough time to get themselves away. As at Breedon (see page 90), the church stands on a hill above the village, there were no adjoining houses to suffer damage and no passers by to be hit by flying stones. Consequently the national press made little of the story then, and it was left to the *Sunday Times*, some five weeks later, to point out the exquisitely ironic timing of the disaster—on Ascension Day in Architectural Heritage Year.

Church towers seldom collapse in this country. Over the last decade or so there seem to have been only two examples, both from Norfolk: the Anglo-Saxon round tower of Morton-on-the-Hill and the nineteenth-century spire at Oxburgh which unfortunately swept away most of the church when it fell, but in the early summer of 1975 flaking masonry from the 700-year-old tower of St Peter's Church was falling into the main street of Inverkeithing in Fife.

It is surprising that the number is not greater. Many of our parish churches have stood for five or six centuries, some for longer. Especially in the more remote areas of the eastern counties, they have to be maintained by villages little more populous than when the church was built at a cost that today would just about restore a mouldering gargoyle. Despite this, abandoned, ruined churches are still a rarity, except in places like Martinthorpe, Great Calceby and Wharram Percy where the villages themselves have completely gone. The odd, unaccountable exceptions, like the ruined church in the quite populous and growing village of Hemington in Leicestershire, are probably outnumbered by the instance of two churches—both often well cared for—sharing the same churchyard in East Anglia.

But the future is not bright. Inflation not only sends the cost of restoration soaring but sews up the pockets of those who would help to meet the cost. Bildeston will have to find something like £50,000 to restore its ruined tower.

The cost of repairing a large town parish church is infinitely greater. The rector of St Mary's, Nantwich, an impressive red-sandstone parish church of a pleasant Cheshire market town, estimates that it will cost £250,000 to safeguard the church for posterity. This is after 25 years of fairly intensive restoration work following a local appeal in the 1950s.

The Bishop of Stepney has given an estimate of £500,000 as the cost of restoring Christ Church, Spitalfields, in the East End of London, though it is fair to say that Ivor Bulmer-Thomas, who knows as much as most people about the care of churches, has described this figure as 'a wild exaggeration'. The fact remains that this masterpiece that Nicholas Hawksmoor, a pupil of Sir Christopher Wren, built between 1723 and 1729, looks more than a little dejected. Large sums of money are obviously needed to restore dignity to this truly magnificent church whose impressive classical portico surmounted by a wide tower and fine octagonal spire looks out across busy Spitalfields market.

Christ Church is one of the most noble examples of the sort of 'down town' parish church most in danger of vanishing, largely because its former residents have already vanished, leaving the parish to the care of industry and commerce which shut up shop in the early evening and have little need for the area on Sundays. Every large town has this problem. Hardly any has managed to solve it without the loss of a church or two, though some redundant churches have been skilfully converted to other uses. Norwich has converted the church of St Peter Hungate, built by the famous Paston family in the fifteenth century, into a museum of ecclesiastical art. St Helen's, Worcester, probably the city's mother church, is now the County Record Office, and not far away the 245ft spire of St Andrew's still serves as a landmark, though the body of the church has gone. Thomas Archer's splendid church of St John's, Smith Square in London, is now the venue for BBC chamber concerts. The parish church at Woodhorn, near Ashington, one of the oldest churches in Northumberland, is to become a museum of the growth of Christianity in the region.

One could go on quoting new uses for old, redundant churches. A few have even been converted into private houses, though not always with the blessing of the practising Church. But in inner, often fading suburbs among tall Victorian villas now converted into seedy flats or sleazy clubs, you will find churches waiting for a call from the demolition men. Not all are worth saving for historical or architectural reasons. But some are. And sometimes even the experts disagree, as they do over the threatened Church of the Holy Trinity, Tunbridge Wells, designed by Decimus Burton in the 1820s. Some people regard this as an architectural monstrosity. Others, led by Sir John Betjeman, love it and want it retained at all cost. In church architecture, as elsewhere, beauty lies in the eyes of the beholder.

There is more unanimity about the beauty of some of the medieval murals that decorate the interior of many a village

34 Church treasures, like this
Saxon frieze at Breedon-on-the-hill,
are costly to maintain

church. The threat to these is usually greater than the threat
to the church fabric. Some are literally vanishing as a result
of age and damp. The wall paintings at Broughton in Buckinghamshire are disintegrating. Those in the same county in the
tiny church of St Nicholas, Little Horwood, showing the patron
saint rescuing small children, are in an almost equally bad state.
They were not improved by the efforts of a sixteenth-century
artist to paint another picture, of the Seven Deadly Sins, over
the top of the earlier work. The Seven Deadly Sins appear again
at Corby Glen in Lincolnshire among what has been called 'one
of the most extensive collections of medieval mural paintings in
the country'. Though this collection was rediscovered and
restored as recently as 1939, it is again said to be 'under threat',
but perhaps not so much as the twelfth century frescoes in the
little early Norman church at Hardham in Sussex. These paintings, amongst the earliest surviving 'visual aids' in England,
were almost certainly the work of Benedictine monks from Lewes
Priory. How long they—and others like them, such as the
fourteenth-century paintings at Chalgrove in Oxfordshire which
are said to be in 'the last stages of decay'—can survive is
doubtful. What is required to save them is a great deal of hard
cash. The £5,000 to £6,000 a year which the Council for Places
of Worship can afford to aid such restoration does not go far
among so many worthy claimants.

This shortage of cash is a permanent worry to those responsible
for the upkeep of our great cathedrals. Canterbury, at the time
of writing, is appealing for £3.5 million and will probably get it.
Cathedrals do not collapse, though Winchester came close to it
a few years ago. The problem of finding enough money to keep
going is great, but no cathedral is likely to vanish, which is
more than can be said for all our parish churches and their
internal treasures, despite the efforts of the Redundant Churches

97

Fund, a kind of national trust for churches, which although founded as recently as 1969, already had 84 parish churches under its care by the spring of 1976.

The large, often handsome and more often wildly impractical, parsonages that the Anglican Church used to build for its clergy in the days when many of them were younger sons of wealthy men and had recourse to sizable private incomes are not so likely to vanish as to change their identity. 'The Old Rectory' is a becoming address on headed notepaper. The Church Commissioners sold 194 parsonages in 1974–5 at an average price of £24,500 each. The new owners must often have spent nearly as much on reconversion, but everybody seems reasonably happy with the results, and the houses are being saved and put to good use.

Stately homes

I wish I could say the same for all our stately homes, but obviously that is impossible. The future for some is looking very sick indeed. For Brough Hall, near Catterick in Yorkshire, for one, it looks as if there may be no future. The house, one of several in the northern counties that were strongholds of Roman Catholicism long after the Reformation in England, has stood empty since 1970, attempts to find a new use for it having failed. In the spring of 1975, the owner, with one eye on a badly leaking roof, applied for permission to demolish most of the Elizabethan central block, including its panelled hall and several stucco friezes, and the Georgian wing, retaining the remaining third of the house as a home for his family. By the time permission was given on 25 November it was too late to repair that roof by the winter. But the delay offers a chance of a reprieve for the Elizabethan block. The owner, forced to drop his previous idea, now sees a possibility that this old core might be retained as an historic monument while the two later wings would have to be demolished. As an eleventh-hour rescue job, this would be better than no Brough at all, but the preservation of the entire house for some useful purpose would be far more satisfying—if it is not already too late.

The need for rapid action to save Stonor Park, Oxfordshire (illustration 35), a house with even more impressive Roman Catholic traditions, is not quite so pressing because £200,000 have been spent on restoration since the end of World War II. In any case, the Stonor time-scale does not lend itself to precipitate action. The house has been occupied by the same family—the Stonors, of course—for over 900 years, which may well be a national record for length of ownership. Having survived the Norman Conquest, the Wars of the Roses, the Civil War, and the pressure of recusant fines that were paid off from the sale of other estates and failed to deter the family from celebrating the mass over the centuries in their fourteenth-century private chapel between the Reformation and Catholic emancipation in 1829, the Stonors have been forced by modern taxation to offer their house for sale. What is offered is essentially a Tudor house in mellow red brick with medieval survivals and eighteenth-century additions, snuggling into the foot of a wooded hill in a 500-acre park, which the present Lord Camoys—the title dates from 1383—a keen naturalist, has turned into a nature reserve where 160 head of fallow deer roam and rare orchids flourish. Four centuries ago, Stonor Park offered sanctuary of another kind. Twelve of the recently canonised English martyrs hid there at one time or another. One was the Jesuit priest, Edmund Campion, who established there a secret printing press, which published his *Decem Rationes.*

Now, as the family moves to the dower house nearby, it is the house and park that seek safety. If no private buyer turns up with the necessary £400,000 that is being asked for the property then there seems a good case for the nation taking over a house of such fine appearance and interesting history and finding some use for it, preferably one which will still allow the public to look over it for much of the year, as they have in the past.

Finding a use for mansions too unwieldy for modern living is

35 Stonor Park near Henley-on-Thames, Oxon, unable to be maintained

obviously a major problem. It is one that has not been solved at Barlaston Hall in Staffordshire. This tall, almost gaunt brick house dating from around 1756, is probably the work of the architect Sir Robert Taylor and has been described as 'one of the best and least altered examples of the compact ingeniously planned country villas which he pioneered.' It was handed to the Wedgwood pottery group as a free gift when the firm bought the Barlaston estate for their new factory and model village shortly before World War II, and was let for a nominal rent to the Bank of England during the war. Since then it has stood empty and neglected, despite attempts by Wedgwoods to find other uses for it. An application to demolish what by then was listed a Grade I building provoked a lengthy, heated debate by correspondence in *The Times* in 1973, and two years later, a Government refusal and an angry response from the group's chairman. There, at the end of 1976, the matter stood. So does the house—just. It would be a shame if what *The Times* called 'one of Britain's finest country houses' just collapsed through neglect.

This seemed likely to be the fate of Hylands House, Writtle, near Chelmsford, unless the district council obtained permission to demolish it themselves. If, as the council said, the house was 'riddled with dry rot and part is in danger of collapsing', demolition seemed a reasonable if regrettable step to take with this listed Georgian mansion in a superb park laid out by Humphrey Repton. But who are the owners who allowed the house to fall into this 'very poor condition'? Surprising as it may or may not be, the council has owned it since 1965, and, according to the Save Britain's Heritage group, has not only 'failed to agree on any plan for using or adapting the house, but it has also rejected at least three offers from outside to restore it'. Now, in the late summer of 1976, the Department of the Environment has rejected demolition on the grounds that the house 'is clearly far from beyond repair', and has suggested to the council ways in which Hylands might be saved.

Not all councils are so little concerned about the future of our historic houses. In that part of County Durham submerged in the new county of Tyne and Wear, both the county and district council are fighting to save Whitburn Hall. This is a rambling, charming architectural hotch-potch of a house standing close by a sycamore-flanked green in one of those unexpectedly attractive villages that have somehow resisted being engulfed by the encircling industrialism. It is one of those houses that 'just growed' between the seventeenth and nineteenth centuries without much thought for architectural purism and the result, if you are not too pedantic about such matters, is wholly delightful. Or it was until 1967. In that year the house became empty and was divided into flats. Twice since, the owners, a Sunderland building firm, have asked permission to demolish the house. Both times they were refused. On the second occasion their knuckles were rapped for having made 'little or any effort to protect a statutorily listed building from vandalism and decay'. As I write, conservation experts from Tyne and Wear Council are examining the building and mulling over possible future uses in response to an 'overwhelming national and local feeling that the hall should be preserved'.

There is much the same feeling about what has rightly been described as 'one of the finest Queen Anne manor houses in East Kent'. This is Ripple House, near Deal, where the Dover council acted promptly in carrying out emergency repairs to a privately owned listed building that had suffered sadly from vandalism since it was bought in 1973 by an Ashford builder who wanted to demolish this gem of a house and build a new one in the grounds.

These smaller manor houses include some of Britain's loveliest buildings, and some of the most vulnerable. Few of them are regularly open to the public and for that reason they are often little known outside their immediate locality, so that, unless, like Sandford Manor, Fulham, they happen to have historic or literary connections, they are liable to be developed under the

100

carpet almost unnoticed. That Sandford Manor was reputedly once the home of Nell Gwynne and later, indisputedly, of Joseph Addison, has not prevented its future from becoming one subject of a prolonged dispute between a developer and Hammersmith council, but it may ensure its restoration and preservation after many years of neglect.

In the absence of an Addison or, particularly, a Nell, there seems less prospect of saving Mickleton Manor, one of a number of listed houses for which an application to demolish was being sought at the end of 1976. I select Mickleton from a roll of numerous houses perhaps equally worthy of saving simply for personal reasons; it happens to have been almost the first Cotswold—or Cotswold-type—manor house I ever saw. I say Cotswold-type because strictly it lies just below the western scarp of the Cotswolds between Stratford and Broadway. It was along the road between those places that I first approached the Cotswolds, caught a glimpse of Mickleton Manor, fell in love with it, and then proceeded to fall equally heavily for almost every other Cotswold manor house. But however fickle one's fancy, one retains a particular sentimental attachment to the first love. And for that selfish reason, I shall feel a special personal sense of loss if Mickleton Manor goes.

The 'if' is quite important. Strong-minded local authorities can, as we have seen, refuse such applications, even when the chances of saving a house seem slight, as with a comparatively small house I know called The Shrubbery, at Aldridge, near Walsall, an area which is something of an industrial jungle. Though the house had been empty for years and the vandals active, the local authority kept its nerve and was suitably rewarded when a firm of architects restored the house, converted it for use as offices and picked up a Civic Trust award.

Paradoxically, this solution, quite right at Aldridge, would

36 Witley Court, Worcestershire, severely damaged by fire, looks forward to renewed life at the core of a country park

be quite wrong at Brunswick Terrace West, Hove. While not quite a 'stately home' in the accepted sense, Brunswick Terrace is a series of homes which could hardly have been statelier when they were built in Regency days. Not now, though, unfortunately. Several of the Grade I listed houses were in a poor state when a developer bought them in 1972 at the height of the property boom. But before he could begin the intended restoration the market collapsed. The only way to cover the cost of restoration was to convert the houses into office use. This was against the policy of the East Sussex County Council who want no extra office space in the Brighton area for the very good reason that the only space for new housing for additional office workers would be on open downland behind the town, too much of which has already been lost. There, four years later, the matter still stands, but at least one house in the terrace may not stand much longer. One possible solution—for the council to buy the houses and do their own restoration—would be unpopular with ratepayers who would have to meet a bill in the region of £250,000. This is no case of a rascally developer or an intransigent council. It is a genuine dilemma. But a solution must soon be found. Those elegant terraces of Brighton and Hove are among the finest sights on the South Coast.

Terrace, town hall and market square

'Elegant' is not perhaps the adjective that springs to mind at the mention of Fleetwood on the Lancashire coast. Yet, why not? There was a good deal of elegance in the resort that Peter Hesketh's drive and capital and Decimus Burton's architectural expertise fashioned in the 1840s to coincide with the completion of the railway line from Euston. What was lacking were the holidaymakers to fill this planned resort, which is why the job was left unfinished. But much of what was built remains intact and ought to be left intact. Unfortunately, there is a proposal to demolish a well preserved group of working-class houses in Flag Street in the sacred cause of 'urban renewal'.

Much the same sort of thing is happening at Frome and Merthyr Tydfil. In the pleasant, narrow-streeted, switchback Somerset town of Frome one of the earliest examples of planned industrial housing in Britain may be lost. In and around Trinity Street about 150 houses built in the seventeenth century for workers in the nearby woollen mills are threatened with demolition. Many are empty and derelict at the time of writing. In the mid-Glamorgan industrial town of Merthyr Tydfil—almost the last place one would expect to find historic buildings—a similar if later group of planned industrial housing, known as The Triangle, may also be demolished if the local council has its way. These houses, built in 1807 by a local ironmaster, comprise all but three of the listed buildings in this unlovely Welsh town. I go along with the local conservationists who believe that both these groups could be modernised, re-occupied and preserved for posterity, as indeed could Flag Street, Fleetwood. If the relevant local authorities want a few tips on this sort of job it would be worth their while travelling to Fife to see what the National Trust for Scotland has done with six seventeenth-century fishermen's houses at Dysart, blended in with five new houses in a former derelict area.

What you do with unwanted town halls, is perhaps a more difficult problem. What the local authorities at Berkhamstead, Buckingham, Tonbridge, Shoreditch and Worksop propose to do with theirs is to pull them down. I doubt if I would sign a petition to save Worksop's but I would be prepared to help man the barricades to keep the demolition people away from the red-brick seventeenth-century town hall at Buckingham. I might even be prepared to climb its clock-tower and cling to the gilded neck of the white swan of Buckingham that looks out across the clean, breezy market square. That, say the local authority, would be unwise, not just because I have no head for heights but because the building is unsafe, which is their excuse for demolition. The Society for Protection of Ancient Buildings, on the other hand, say that the building is quite sound. If it is, and I respect their opinion, then the building must be saved at all costs. Buckingham is one of my favourite small towns: a delightfully unspoilt agricultural town with its sheep and cattle market strung out along its main street; an unsophisticated town, poles apart in atmosphere from the gin-and-tonicky commuter towns at the southern end of its county. I wouldn't like to see a brick of it disturbed, and I go along with the Save Britain's Heritage people in saying that to demolish that town hall would be 'a singular act of vandalism'.

Even finer than Buckingham's market square is the one at Newark-on-Trent, which Sir Nikolaus Pevsner found 'a joy to examine'. That joy is hardly unconfined at the moment because its oldest building is in a poor state of repair. This building is a former coaching inn, the Old White Hart, that Pevsner described as 'one of the paramount examples of fourteenth-century, timber-framed, domestic architecture in England'. Unhappily, it has been described by the local council's architect as totally unsafe, and it is likely to deteriorate further unless landlord and tenant stop arguing about who pays for the repairs. If they do not settle their dispute soon, the local council will have to step in and do the job, but that will mean postponing other important improvement schemes.

Public houses

Too many pubs have been ruined internally by brewers who tart them up for the benefit of the assumed tastes of the spirit-drinking devil they hope to know in place of the beer-drinking devil they do know, and a number of good Edwardian and Victorian town-centre pubs have vanished in the urban redevelopment holocaust. The Wellington and The Manchester Arms in central Manchester—by the skin of their teeth and the enthusiasm of local conservationists—and the Barton Arms in Birmingham seem to have kept their licences when all around were losing theirs. But there is some anxiety about the White Horse at Beverley, which has just changed hands. There is something slightly sinister about the statement by the new owners, Samuel Smith of Tadcaster, that they will *try* (my italics) to preserve as much as they can of this old coaching inn, parts of which are 500 years old. If they fail to try very hard indeed, there will be trouble on Humberside, where Nellie's, as the pub is locally known, is something of an institution.

But even institutions can vanish, as the citizens of Bradford discovered recently when the Kirkgate market hall was swept away to make way for a new shopping centre and market. Perhaps the echoes of the howl of rage that went up then in Yorkshire accents may linger on long enough in the North and Midlands to save these vast temples of trade that the Victorians usually opened with massed choirs singing the *Messiah* to strike the right sort of religious fervour that was considered suitable for trade in those parts. Built mainly of glass and iron, like the exquisite shopping arcades that came in with the last of the same tide of building fashion, their market halls owed their architectural inspiration to those country house conservatories, like Paxton's Great Conservatory and Lily House at Chatsworth, that led, via his Crystal Palace, to the seaside piers and great railway stations, both now threatened species.

Piers

The seaside pier is a delicate-looking monument to the Victorian architect at his unexpectedly light-hearted best. It evolved from a simple landing stage for venturesome seaborne trippers to a dashing seaward extension of the promenade along which, as Nathaniel Hawthorne, the American writer, observed at Southport in 1857, 'the visitors perambulate to and fro without any imaginable object'. Eventually it developed into the sort of amusement centre that was indispensable to every fully fledged seaside resort, except for an exclusive minority like Scarborough and Whitby that clung, in deliberate disdain of the new trends, to the traditional spa assembly room.

37   Clevedon pier, not renewed since it broke in two in 1970

This process of evolution fitted neatly into the nineteenth century. In 1800, the pier was still in its pre-historic era. By 1900 it had fully matured and was adorned by its full fine foliage of pavilions, tea rooms and penny-consuming slot machines where one could control a football match, witness an execution, or satisfy one's curiosity about what the butler saw. The 1860s was the peak decade of 'pier mania', and, except for the addition of a Moorish Pavilion here and a Floral Hall there, little further building was done after the turn of the century.

Only about 54 of Britain's piers remain, and not all of those are in one piece. Clevedon pier (illustration 37)—Ian Nairn's tip as 'probably the best Victorian pier in Britain'—has been in two parts since 1970. Saltburn had its pier head washed away about 1974. Of the others, Cromer suffered damage in the great gale of 2 January, 1976, two days after Brighton's West pier was closed because its owners consider it no longer safe.

The trouble is that after a century of the corrosive effect of salt water on iron legs many piers are proving to be as delicate as they look. Public taste has changed too. 'Pier Follies' are no longer the draw they were fifty years ago and most people can now guess what the butler saw. With a few notable exceptions, where their owners have kept abreast of the times, the turnstiles in those Oriental domed entrance kiosks no longer click often enough to pay for the rising cost of maintenance, let alone make a profit.

Demolition, it seems to some owners—often but not invariably local councils—is the only way to cut losses. Brighton's West pier, built in 1866 to the design of that most prolific of pier engineers Eugenius Burton, has faced this threat, and much lively, well-publicised opposition to it, for some years. New Brighton pier, on which the then unknown Beatles once performed for thirty shillings a night, faces demolition. Saltburn pier, after being offered for sale for one new penny to anyone who would guarantee to restore it, is similarly threatened. The sea may demolish the piers at Hunstanton and Teignmouth if repairs are not soon carried out, while there is some danger that Bognor's may be developed out of recognition. Britain's longest pier, at Southend, is being preserved simply because demolition would be a more costly alternative.

Piers may not be the attraction they once were to the holiday-makers, but to allow them to disappear would look like an admission of defeat in resorts like Saltburn, which has already lost another eccentric Victorian structure, its Ha'penny Bridge. Conservationists and nostalgists, which includes most of us, regret the threat to these essentially British eccentricities just as they regret the threat to our great London railway termini. Of these, Euston, a mixture of cathedral and stately home, has gone, the threat to St Pancras has been temporarily averted, but Liverpool Street is in jeopardy, along with its adjoining enormous station hotel, the Great Eastern, and their semi-derelict, down-at-heel, next-door neighbour, Broad Street Station.

The Railways

I must admit that Liverpool Street fails to thrill me as St Pancras does, perhaps because I seem to have spent half my life popping in and out of St Pancras, and nearly ended it there when the coffee stall I had just left for the safety of the cellars stopped a German bomb. It is perhaps also because my local patriotism is always enflamed by the sight of that superb train-shed, built in my native county of Derbyshire and once boasting the largest single-span roof in the world. Thinking of St Pancras, I cannot agree with Sir John Betjeman's view that Liverpool Street 'is London's most picturesque terminus'. There is too much mess, too much grime, too much inconvenience, and—whenever I use it—too much rain. But it has something; the original train-sheds of 1874, designed, by Edward Wilson, 'like a gothic cathedral or iron and glass', in Mark Giroud's words, for one thing; those cherubic porters, signalmen and stokers embossed in terracotta above the walkway by which you enter from Bishopgate, for another.

The Great Eastern has its triumphs too. It contains, as Betjeman, Giroud and a drawing-board of equally distinguished architects and critics agreed in a letter to *The Times*, 'some of the most spectacular Victorian and Edwardian interiors in London'. Among those interiors are an art-nouveau glass-domed dining room with dancing sylphs; lots of Italianate plasterwork and two impressively decorated Masonic Halls, one Egyptian, the other Greek.

Poor, neglected Broad Street cannot compete with such magnificence and did not need to, as it was there first, being built in 1866 as the terminus of the humble suburban North London railway. But it had—if the pun is forgivable—architectural ideas above its station. Some of these survive above the modern façade, notably the French Renaissance twin mansard pavilions, while at one side, almost hidden behind later clutter, is a fine Florentine stairway, leading now, unhappily, to bare, unromantic platforms.

All this site, except for the Abercorn Rooms of the Great Eastern Hotel, British Rail propose to clear. This is too drastic. While few obscurants would wish to retain the entire complex untouched, there is an alternative scheme, prepared by the Liverpool Street Station Campaign, that would blend the best of the old buildings with some admittedly necessary new ones.

Because railway stations were designed by men rightly convinced that they were helping to inaugurate a transportation revolution, they display Victorian architecture at its confident best. All over the provinces there are decaying stations crying out to be preserved, like G. T. Andrews's now derelict classical station at Market Weighton, on the Yorkshire Wolds, for use if possible, or as historical monuments if not. Among them is the oldest passenger station in the world, Liverpool Road, Manchester. Opened with appropriate pomp by the Duke of Wellington on 15 September 1830, it was closed to passenger traffic less ostentatiously in 1844. Today, though the only Grade I listed building in Manchester apart from the cathedral, it stands in what has been described as 'a terrible state of disrepair'. Used until recently as the headquarters of a railway goods yard, this former terminus of the Liverpool and Manchester Railway demands restoration and use as a railway museum.

Near the other end of the Liverpool and Manchester Railway, stands—just—Edge Hill, thought to be the oldest non-terminus station still in working order, and almost certainly the first junction, handling goods traffic from the Wapping and Waterloo tunnels and passengers from Lime Street. Standing in an area on which demolition has laid a heavy clumsy hand, Edge Hill was condemned to share this fate and to be replaced by a halt, but a reprieve arrived just in time in 1974 to allow the interested authorities to look again at its future. One promising suggestion is that the 1836 part of the station might be restored and the Wapping Tunnel cutting to what little remains of Crown Street Station reopened as a history trail.

Farther north, Windermere, the Lake District's last surviving rail terminus still in use, has become a squalid slum of cracked, peeling walls and broken gas lamps that gives visitors an unhappy introduction to one of Britain's loveliest areas. Though it looks as if a gale might easily sweep it away, it is not yet scheduled for demolition. This is not the case of Bridgend in Glamorgan, apart from Chepstow the last original station surviving from Brunel's Swansea line of 1850, and Neath, which dates from 1877 and was one of the first stations to be built after the Great Western decided to conform to standard gauge. Also due for demolition is the old station at Newmarket, built in 1848

38 The imperfect state of 'the most perfect of all station buildings' at South Wingfield, Derbyshire

107

by a 'third-rate architect or some kind of crank', according to the local council, but much admired by railway enthusiasts and lovers of the bizarre.

There is nothing bizarre about Francis Thompson's 1840 station at South Wingfield in Derbyshire (illustration 38)—except its present state. This 'most perfect of all station houses,' in Christian Barman's words, stands derelict in a sordid sea of flotsam and jetsam cast up, apparently, by the National Coal Board. It would, like so many station buildings, have lent itself admirably to conversion into a private house, were it not for the sleep-killing roar of trains on the still busy Inter-City line between St Pancras, Derby and Sheffield. As it is, what is possibly the last survivor of the stations that Thompson built so superbly for the Hudson–Stephenson North Midland Railway may enjoy a new life as an exhibit on the Midland Railway Trust's 'museum' line between Butterley and Pye Bridge.

Besides the stations, other pieces of finely designed railway furniture are in danger. One of these, in a modified pier/market hall style of architecture, is the now disused Great Northern railway bridge that crosses Georgian Friar Gate, Derby. Cast iron was the material used in its construction, but the tracery is so delicate that it might well have been woven in lace. When the now-defunct local firm of Handyside built the bridge in 1878 there were indignant letters to the local press from conservationists who objected to what they described as 'the best street in Derby being desecrated by this monstrosity'. But Derby has learned to appreciate its bridge. When there was talk of removing it a few years ago to make way for a stronger new bridge to carry the inner ring road there were similar letters protesting at this desecration. In the event, the bridge was saved —temporarily—by economy cuts. But, sometime, the danger will arise again.

Some miles farther east along the same long-abandoned branch line one of the longest and finest surviving viaducts on the old Great Northern may vanish if British Rail has its way. This viaduct may lack the superbly delicate tracery of the Derby bridge, but what it does have is a most graceful curve on which it sweeps for 500yd across the industrialised Erewash Valley and the Nottinghamshire boundary, not five miles from D. H. Lawrence's birthplace at Eastwood. Local authorities on both sides of the boundary are anxious to retain what is one of the few listed buildings in this architectural desert. But there is the usual problem of money for restoration, and there is the savagely ironic possibility that the viaduct could disappear in 1977, its centenary year.

Canals

Another and, in its own way, equally delightful transport building could disappear at any time through neglect. This is the cylindrical, three-storeyed cottage alongside the Thames & Severn Canal not far from the Gloucestershire village of Coates

and near to the eastern end of the Sapperton Tunnel. This was one of five so-called 'round houses' built by the canal company in 1799 for the lock-keepers and lengthmen. Spaced out at intervals along the 29 miles of canal they served, in Christopher Powell's words, 'as a series of architectural exclamation marks'. Two others were built on the Staffordshire & Worcestershire Canal. One at Gailey Lock (illustration 39) is still intact, but the other near Stourton Junction is in ruins. The Coates round house, enriched by warm Cotswold stone walls and pointed gothic windows, still looks restorable—and well worth the effort and cost.

39 Well-preserved canal round-house at Gailey Lock Staffordshire

Farm buildings

It is easy, as I know to my cost, to confuse Coates with Richard Jefferies's village of Coate, some twenty miles to the south-east, near Swindon. The birthplace, Coate Farm, and its outbuildings are in a fairly advanced stage of decay, and a national appeal to save them was launched in the summer of 1975. Parts of the farmhouse date from 1700, but the outbuildings were erected by Jefferies's father, mainly by his own hands, about 1840. The story of how Richard wrote while his father, understandingly, toiled until he was ruined, has often been told, but is worth repeating. Lovers of Richard Jefferies's writing will feel that his father's sacrifice was rewarded, but it would be a pity if the tangible reminders of that story had to be sacrificed through lack of funds.

If the interest in the Coate Farm buildings lies mainly in their literary connections, there are two other endangered farm buildings that ought to be saved for their beauty and historic interest. Both are tithe barns. One at Middle Littleton in Worcestershire dates from the mid-thirteenth century. It has eleven bays, and one survivor of its original pair of waggon porches. The other, at Coggeshall in Essex, is a century older still and may have been the grange barn of a Cistercian abbey founded by King Stephen about 1140, just about 200 years before the birth of Geoffrey Chaucer. Another 630 or so years later, scenes from Chaucer's *Canterbury Tales* were shot in that same barn for the great Italian film maker, Passolini, who was murdered not long afterwards.

Both barns are, at that time of writing, near to collapse. Both have friends trying to raise enough money to repair them, and the National Trust has agreed to take over the Middle Littleton barn when—or if—the money is raised.

A miscellany—Electric Palace to Banbury Cross

Not all the buildings that need to be saved are as old as those two. The Grand Theatre at Blackpool dates only from 1894 and may not look particularly impressive externally. But its auditorium is, in the words of a Department of the Environment inspector, 'a splendid example of ornate, opulent Victorian theatre building whose exuberance and panache is undimmed even by its present indifferent decoration and lighting system'. Unfortunately, the future of this interior is uncertain. Its owners want to alter it drastically, after an initial application for demolition had been rejected. A lot of people, including, to hardly anyone's surprise, Sir John Betjeman, feel that it is 'irreplaceable, the true architecture of entertainment, and it must be saved and used as a theatre again'. And why not? It was so used until 1972 and playing to good houses. As the inspector said, 'Such an accomplished expression of the architectural and social history of the late nineteenth century must not be lightly destroyed', especially as the Grand is one of the last surviving examples of the work of Frank Matcham, an outstanding theatre architect of his day.

Lacking the 'exuberance and panache' of the Grand's auditorium, is the Electric Palace, Harwich, that the DOE has listed 'for sociological interest' because it 'is one of the oldest purpose-built cinemas in England'. It was built in eighteen weeks in 1811 to the design of Harold R. Hooper of Ipswich for Charles Thurston, a travelling showman, whose 'Royal Travelling Picture Show' had been appearing on East Anglian greens periodically from the turn of the century. In his travelling days, Thurston had used a marquee for his show, and his Electric Palace shows evidence of its ancestry. 'In essence,' wrote David Robinson in *The Times* newspaper, 'it is a large brick tent, with an ornate facade of flimsy construction, generously decorated with plaster

110

swags and wreaths, all dominated by a plaque proclaiming the year of opening.' The year of its abrupt closure—1956—is not shown. For sixteen years after that it stood empty, its side-street position camouflaging it from keen-eyed developers. Then, when it was about to be demolished in 1972 to make space for a car park, there were local protests, official listing and the formation of a trust to raise the money for restoration. It is not saved yet, but its chances are fairly good.

Eyebrows may rise at the preservation of a cinema. Why? Any good example of a class of building that has played a significant part in the social life of the nation is worth saving, and for my generation, born in World War I, much of our social life was centred on the cinema.

But where do we stop? If we are going to preserve cinemas, why not those buildings euphemistically called 'public conveniences'? And why not, indeed, if they are as good of their kind as the dignified Edwardian-Classical ladies' lavatory at Herne Bay in Kent, which the local council want to demolish because they say it is unsafe, and the Save Britain's Heritage group want to preserve because of its splendid Classical architecture.

After this, it can hardly be surprising to know that some people would like to save a threatened mill-chimney. It is at Middleton in Lancashire and may be the tallest in England, even since the top 40ft of its original 358ft have been removed for

40   The fate of Temple Bar still hangs in the balance

safety reasons. Built with $1\frac{1}{2}$ million bricks in the 1840s, it has become a landmark with the same sort of sentimental appeal for Middleton people that the Wrekin has for Salopians, which explains why its owners, having no further commercial use for it, would rather sell it for £5 to someone who will preserve it than see it demolished.

There was time when Temple Bar (illustration 40) meant as much to Londoners though, in a particularly iconoclastic period in our history, they seem to have uttered no murmur of dissent when it was demolished in 1879 after it and its only predecessor had guarded the approach to the City from Westminster for some 600 years. The original Temple Bar, which probably dated from the late thirteenth century, was replaced in 1673 by a 'dignified and elegant' archway in Portland Stone over which was a small room that was used for many years by Child's Bank to store their ledgers. Above that were fixed three tall iron spikes on which the heads of traitors were placed from time to time to discourage any intending emulators. The last heads to appear there were those of rebels in the '45 Rebellion. Later the Bar began to lose some of its appeal, especially among those who had to drive through the narrow arch, and its removal was only prevented by a single vote in Common Council in 1787. Almost a century later, the decision was reversed, the Bar pulled down and its stones deposited in a Faringdon Road yard.

But that is not the end of the Temple Bar story. Some ten years later, the stones were given to Sir Henry Meux, who reassembled the Bar as a gateway to his estate at Theobald's Park near Waltham Cross. There—and this may surprise a good many Londoners—it still stands, though fenced in and inaccessible to the public except for the vandals who are hastening the disintegration that neglect had started. The Society for the Protection of Ancient Buildings have been looking for an alternative site, which should surely be in London. Perhaps, as the Department of the Environment has accepted, a new site within the grounds of St Paul's Cathedral would be as good a place as any to re-erect this 'noble monument of architecture', as Dickens put it, which was almost certainly the work of that noblest of English architects, Sir Christopher Wren.

To my mind, a much less noble monument is the ornate memorial to Prince Albert in the square named after him in Manchester. But Manchester people—and manifestly their pigeons—have a great affection for the statue, and what Manchester thinks today ought not be disregarded by its city council who have samefully neglected poor Albert over the years. A report a year over the last 24 years has commented with increasing acidity on the poor state of the monument, erected in 1869, and has drawn attention during that period to the removal on safety grounds of four pinnacles, three female figures and sundry pieces of carved masonry. Without the aid of another architect's report, it is easy to see evidence of further decay. The memorial, and the imposing Town Hall close by, have always symbolised for me the sober dignity and prosperity of Manchester. But if I were a Mancunian, I would now be a bit worried that the memorial at least might be symbolic of decay.

And where would Banbury be without its cross? Banbury cakes and Banbury Cross symbolise this busy little Oxfordshire town just as Albert Square symbolises Manchester. The cakes, I trust, are not in danger; the cross is. There has been much talk lately of removing it because it is a traffic hazard. The present cross is neither particularly old—1859—nor particularly handsome, but because it is bound up with our earliest memories of nursery-rhyme ladies on white horses it means a lot not only to Banbury folk but to English-speaking people everywhere. And many people who have never been to Banbury must feel that if it is in the way of traffic then it is the traffic rather than the cross that should give way. Those who do know this Cotswold-stone town would say that Banbury has lost too much of its antiquity already and ought to fight like mad to keep what is left.

That goes, too, for all the other buildings mentioned in this chapter and a lot more that there is not the space to mention. As 1976 drew to a close, more than fifty applications to demolish listed buildings were being considered. Not all will be approved; some may be. Can we afford to lose any of our dwindling stock of listed buildings?

Caravans at Towyn, Clwyd

113

8 Reclamation and Restoration

Staffordshire success story

So far, I have painted a rather gloomy picture of crumbling buildings and hedgeless fields where 'spring more resembles winter now than spring'; a Britain degenerating into a wasteland where 'no birds sing'. 'Change and decay in all around I see,' but I also see some hopeful signs that all is not yet lost. As Oliver Edwards endearingly remarked to Dr Johnson, 'I have tried too in my time to be a philosopher; but I don't know how, cheerfulness was always breaking in'.

It was at Stoke-on-Trent, of all unlikely places, that cheerfulness broke in for me. On a grey, misty, autumn afternoon it is not a place that normally radiates good cheer. Dante's *Inferno*, I used to think, must have looked like Stoke on such a day when smoke from those innumerable rows of identical bottle-kilns wreathed above the city unable to force a way through the cloud belt and mingled with those other smoke columns that rose from the smouldering grey mountains of slag. But Stoke, like most of Britain, is changing. Unlike most of Britain, it is changing for the better.

The smoke has gone. So have the bottle-kilns, or most of them; almost too many of them, for we need a few reminders of Arnold Bennett's Stoke. Most of the slag heaps have gone too, and that is a big improvement, as is the disappearance of most of those ugly pits from which the clay marl for potteries was once dug. Some heaps have actually been tipped into the holes, a happy arrangement which disposes of two evils for the price of one.

The fact is that Stoke is undergoing a huge face-lift. It was very necessary because the city has more derelict land within its boundaries than any other local authority in England. At the end of World War II, nearly 2,500 acres was officially derelict land. By the sumer of 1976 the figure had dropped to about 1,600 but that still represented more than seven per cent of the entire city.

But some astonishing things have happened to reduce those figures still further. In the best fairy-tale tradition, three ugly sisters have turned into Central Forest Park. The sisters were slag heaps. One has now vanished and the others have been

landscaped. Where slag once smouldered, there are ski slopes, a nature reserve, picnic areas, camp site, a flower garden and a golf course. Elsewhere a spoil heap fitted perfectly into a marl hole at its foot. Housing and light industry now cover the 70 acre site. Another marl pit has become a sports arena. A bog of of polluted water between the canal and the main railway line has been cleaned up and turned into an already popular water sports centre. These new parks are being linked by Greenways, traffic-free walks along the 13 miles of disused railway line that used to serve Bennett's 'Five Towns' (and the sixth he ignored). Of course none of this makes Stoke into a beauty spot, but if you knew it 30 years ago, you will agree that wonders have been performed.

More wonders have been performed at the other end of Staffordshire, about an hour's drive south of Stoke, where in 1956 the then Brownhills Urban District Council bought a 230 acre canal reservoir and the wasteland surrounding it. This unpromising area of industrial dereliction enclosed within a loop railway line just north of the Roman Watling Street—now the A5—has become the Chasewater water sports and leisure centre, a tremendous attraction for all those Midlanders who like just messing about in boats and for the even greater number who enjoy watching the inland sailors just messing about at their 'sky-blue trades'. It has been an astonishing transformation; an object lesson not only in converting a moribund landscape into a living one but also in killing two unpleasant birds with one stone by dumping fly ash from Midland power stations and collieries in the foundations of the reshaped terrain.

Industrial revolution in reverse

As I saw in a single misty autumn afternoon, the Staffordshire landscape is changing for the better—in both the Potteries of the north and the Black Country of the south—almost as rapidly as it changed for the worse in the nineteenth century. This sort of industrial revolution in reverse is taking place in other parts of Britain also. As long ago as 1952, Lancashire planners began a major facial operation on a particularly devastated area in the Makerfield district south of Wigan, where nearly 2,000 acres of barren ground was littered with the rotting carcass of dead industries. Within a year, an 11 acre, 60ft naked spoil heap of a long disused colliery had been clothed with 15,000 young trees —mainly alders and corsican pine—that form today a nearly-mature woodland.

The total cost of this minor preliminary operation was £653; about the price of a ticket for Concorde's maiden flight. For the sort of money that a second division Football League club would expect to pay for a moderately experienced reserve goalkeeper— £17,000—the planners then turned a squalid trough of industrial left-overs called Whalley's Basin into a sports ground with four

42 Once a water-logged waste, Westport Water Park is now Stoke-on-Trent's main outlet for water-based recreation

football pitches, a cricket ground, bowling green and running track before moving on to what the locals called the 'Black Alps' and what the late John Barr, in *Derelict Britain*, called 'a loathsome mountainscape of spoil tips and an enormous and treacherous flash'. Its name on the map is Bryn Hall. Today, after the removal of a million tons of spoil from its 180 acres, it is pasture land speckled with spinneys.

Across the Pennines in the Parkinson–Trueman area of the South Yorkshire coalfield, similar rescue work is going on around places like Swinton, Maltby, Pontefract and Wath-on-Dearne. A few miles away to the north-west, anglers now catch trout beneath the shade of two cooling towers in a 35-acre fishery called Cromwell Lake that was formed by joining together three disused gravel pits, while alongside the A1 a flock of 18 arctic tern are among the 200 different species of birds that have visited the Fairburn Ings nature reserve and bird sanctuary that is an oasis in a desert of colliery spoil heaps.

It would be foolish to claim for any of these areas, or the rather similar ones in Northumberland and Durham, and along the Erewash and Rother valleys of east Derbyshire and west Nottinghamshire, that the Loathley Lady of industry has turned into Princess Charming overnight, or even in a decade. The Black Country may now be a darkish shade of grey, but a visitor to any of the areas I have mentioned would consider 'drab' a somewhat euphemistic adjective to describe them. Even the native who appreciates the changes—and there are some who, like Ian Nairn, mourn the passing of the familiar mountains of spoil—would claim no more than that his area has become less ugly than it was. Time is a great reclaimer, but you need plenty of it; the coal, iron and steel industries, and those miscellaneous industries that grew up around them, threw out enough refuse to keep even nature busy for a century in covering them completely.

Given that sort of time, though, even the worst industrial excrescences do just go away. Alongside the Staffordshire & Worcestershire Canal near Kinver, in that area where the two counties become inextricably mixed up, I explored an attractive stretch of woodland containing odd grassy mounds which on closer inspection turned out to be composed of slag from an ironworks that flourished on the site in the eighteenth century. In the pleasant, if curiously named, Eureka Park at Swadlincote in south Derbyshire, I was asked to guess why a large ring of grass wore a different shade of green from the surrounding lawn. Thoughts of fairy-rings were quickly dispelled when I was told that it indicated the position of an infilled shaft of the former Eureka Colliery that had given the park both its habitation and its name.

Something more akin to instant beauty may be expected, however, when reclamation has finished at Shipley Park, some 30 miles north-east of Swadlincote, on the edge of the Erewash Valley. Once it was the private park of the wealthy Miller

Mundy family. Then the miners came to the edge of the park, the family left, and the mansion became a ruin that was eventually demolished. The mines closed, and reclamation began. But before paradise could be restored, the colliers came back, this time to scratch the surface for open-cast coal. Now that too has finished; the Derbyshire County Council is busy on restoration, and very soon paradise will be regained, and the area will be opened to the public as a country park.

Reclamation in Wales

Equally rapid results are being claimed by the Wales Tourist Board for the southern part of its area. It may be a bit early to be tempting tourists to look for beauty in the Valleys, as its leaflets are doing, but certainly a big change is coming over this once coal-begrimed corner of Britain. How green now is the valley of Gilfach Goch, the setting of Richard Llewellyn's best-selling novel of 1939, since the rotting remains of four or five coal mines and various drift workings have been removed, and replaced by grass and trees. Some twenty miles, and perhaps as many valleys, farther east there is a new trout leap in the stream by a red-painted bridge at Abercarn that seems to symbolise a more cheerful future for industrial South Wales. Because the valley floors were usually too narrow to accommodate more than one industry at a time, and because the natural beauty of the enclosing mountains remained largely untainted, the valleys lend themselves better than most other blighted areas to quick trans-formation from black to green. The Wales Tourist Board may be pushing its luck a bit now, but another twenty years could make a lot of difference.

New uses for Nottinghamshire gravel workings

That sort of time is generally sufficient to turn disused gravel workings into something attractive, useful, or both. Sometimes the transformation is even more rapid. At Attenborough, on the western outskirts of Nottingham, the Nottinghamshire Trust for Nature Conservation set up its first nature reserve, in an extensive network of old gravel workings alongside the river Trent, in the early 1960s. This area of reed swamp, marshland dotted with ancient willows, rough grassland and an archipelago of small islands is now rich in wildlife and beauty. A view of the village, with its characteristic Nottinghamshire stumpy spire rising above the white-fronted, red-pantiled riverside houses in the fading light of a summer's evening would have delighted Peter de Wint, who, more than any other artist, captured the quiet charm of the Trent valley.

A few miles farther down that valley, on the other side of Nottingham at Holme Pierrepont, 225 acres of gravel workings in pleasant surroundings have been converted into a magnificent multi-purpose water-sports centre and country park, which has already become an international rowing centre. A similar centre for power boat enthusiasts has been created from equally un-promising gravel workings at South Cerney, near Cirencester in the Cotswolds.

Power boats may scare birds away, but in general such reclaimed sheets of water are not long in attracting wildlife. Reeds colonise the shallow water near the edges of the new lakes, soon providing breeding sites for insects and warblers. The shingly terrace on the edge of the pools is likely to attract waders. A rare visitor to Britain before World War II, the ringed plover, now builds its patchy nest in the terraces of numerous gravel pits in the Home Counties, as Richard Mabey has pointed out in *The Unofficial Countryside*. Nor are they the only birds of these waters. The swifts come, attracted by the midges, and so do the sand martins, the wagtails, and, most exciting of all, what Mabey calls 'our most exotic native water bird, the great crested grebe'. There was a time in the mid-nineteenth century when the dictates of ladies' fashions led to the almost complete extinction of these birds, whose ruffs ornamented garden party hats and whose skins were demanded for muffs. Saved by the Bird Protection Act of 1869 and by changes in fashion, their population has undoubtedly increased, though the present total is uncertain. What is certain is that almost every island site of five acres or more in a disused gravel pit is likely to have at least one resident pair of grebes.

Quarry Nature Reserve

The scars of quarrying take much longer to hide than those inflicted by gravel workings, but they can sometimes offer some consolation in their desolation by offering new habitats for wild-life. Given the right set of circumstances, an interesting flora can quickly spring up on the floor of a disused limestone quarry. Orchids, particularly, like such spots. More than 300 flower spikes of the bee orchid were counted in a single redundant Peak District quarry in 1971, admittedly an outstandingly productive year, and only a few less in a neighbouring quarry. Several species of orchid, and numerous other plants, have colonised the series of quarries and waste-heaps in Millers Dale that were abandoned about 1930 and were acquired in 1974 by Derbyshire Naturalists' Trust as a nature reserve. This trust has already converted a miscellaneous collection of limestone quarries, gravel pits, limeyards, brickyards and other man-made holes into attractive and scientifically valuable nature reserves, and most other county trusts can point to similar rescue operations in the most unlikely places.

To say that something can be saved from a wreck is not to offer an excuse for causing the wreck in the first place. The kestrels, jackdaws and occasional little owls that rest on the quarry faces in Millers Dale may be just a tiny remnant of the flocks of birds that flew above the Dale before the quarrymen came with their explosives and their machinery. Though a rich variety of plants and mammals have found new homes in and

119

43 Abbeydale Industrial Hamlet, Sheffield, before restoration

around the quarries, they may represent smaller and different varieties from those that were there when this was virgin ground. Though the quarry floor is acquiring a carpet of green, it still looks like a quarry working, not a particularly pretty thing.

Cumbria steelworks reclaimed

To praise some of the reclamation work that has been going along the coast of Cumbria between St Bees Head and Maryport is not to say that this coast is as beautiful as it must have been three centuries ago, or even to deny that much of that coastline is still a squalid mess. But it would be equally foolish to deny that there have been some improvements in the last decade. It is an area with an interesting history. Workington was once Gabrosentum, the site of a Roman fort. In the ninth century it sheltered the Lindisfarne monks, trying to escape from the Danes to Ireland with their precious Lindisfarne Gospels, as later it sheltered Mary, Queen of Scots, for a night in 1568 after the battle of Langside. Much more recently it became a steel centre, with all the attendant litter that this implies. Its white cliffs are formed not by chalk but man-made slag and any blue-birds flying over them are liable to take on an off-black hue. But it is changing. A coal tip the same size and shape as the Stepped Pyramid, 198ft, has been cut down to hillock size; a devastated area covering 135 acres has been landscaped. Girls in jodhpurs ride ponies where once trucks tipped slag, and the only holes in the ground are the 18 on the new golf course which has been laid out on this former wasteland. At Harrington, just to the north, there is grassland where there were slag-heaps and neat yachts in the former coal dock.

Farther south, nearer to St Bees Head, Whitehaven is an altogether more distinguished town that had begun to look as if it might be extinguished. A comparative upstart compared with Workington, it was a hamlet until Sir John Lowther planned a

120

new seaport and coal-mining town there about 1690. Sir James Lowther—later first Earl of Lonsdale—continued the good work throughout most of the eighteenth century. Good work it really was. A century ago Whitehaven must have been one of the most delightful Georgian towns in Britain, with a few Jacobean houses surviving. But towards the end of the eighteenth century the coal trade began to decline and the port became too small for the newer, larger ships. Whitehaven became a depressed town. Since World War II, many—too many—of its decayed old houses have been demolished. But that nonsense has now stopped. The entire town centre has become a conservation area. Surviving old houses are being restored and made habitable again. The slow slide to senility has been arrested. Whitehaven will remain an industrial town—quite rightly, as it was born out of industry—but it is becoming worth visiting for its own sake, and as a reasonable centre for those people who want a breath of sea air with their exploration of nearby Lakeland.

Small town successes

From the opposite corner of England, Faversham in Kent, there is an equally heartening story of a slightly smaller town that has saved itself, mainly by its own exertions. Faversham is not widely known for its charm, partly, I suppose, because one does not expect to find much of aesthetic value between the Medway towns and the Thanet coast, and partly because people have been inclined to accept it at its own valuation as a workaday town. Yet since the time of Defoe, who was shocked because its growing wealth sprang from smuggling and owling (the illegal export of wool), the guide book writers have usually had kind words for it. Even Cobbett, whose lively pen was often dipped in vitriol, called it 'a very pretty little town', and eventually the townsfolk got the message. Inspired by some prodding from the Society for the Protection of Ancient Buildings, who persuaded

121

the council to buy the fine half-timbered, sixteenth-century Arden's House—home of a former mayor who was murdered by his wife and her lover—instead of pulling it down, by the arrival of a new town clerk with conservationist leanings, and by the replacement of two good buildings by a supermarket and some shops that looked as out of place as a bunny girl at the Atheneum, the locals formed a Faversham Society to protect their town from further unfortunate development.

The Society has had some defeats. It could not prevent the demolition of the Georgian St Ann's House, for instance, and it achieved no more than an honourable draw in finding a buyer for the sixteenth-century barn at Davington Court who had it removed for re-erection at Edenbridge on the other side of the county.

But it has had some notable victories too. It saved the six-teenth-century Fleur de Lys inn and is converting it as the Society's headquarters, information centre and museum. It saved the eighteenth-century Chart Gunpowder Mill, the oldest of its kind in the world, and may have it restored to working order and open to the public by the time this book is published. Thanks to the Society, an open, untamed area between the town and the River Swale is to retain its character, a proposed new road scheme through the town centre has at least been halted, and some streets in the centre have, belatedly, been closed to traffic. It now seems likely that this pleasant, breezy little town will enter the twenty-first century almost unscathed.

King's Lynn took up this 'do-it-yourself' conservation policy even earlier than Faversham, and long before conservation had become a socially acceptable word, perhaps because it has more

45 A preserved and converted lighthouse at Portland Bill, Dorset

buildings worth saving than most other towns of its size in Britain, which may surprise people who know it only for its annual Festival or for its almost perpetual traffic jams. But a few hundred yards north of that stationary wall of traffic is what John Seymour, in his excellent *Companion Guide to East Anglia,* has rightly called 'the most romantic town in England'. With its two fine churches, two market places, two magnificent guildhalls, several good inns and Henry Bell's Customs House of 1683 that I consider the most charming small secular building in England, King's Lynn has probably more fine public buildings than any other town of comparable size in England. If that were not enough for this town which is comparatively unknown to tourists, it has numerous fine merchants' houses and warehouses as a reminder that it was once England's second-busiest port. It was to save these, rather than the already well preserved public buildings, that the King's Lynn Preservation Trust was set up.

To see what it has done, you have only to look at Hampton Court, almost a merchant's town in itself, with counting house, warehouses and apprentices' quarters adjoining the mansion itself. When I first saw it in the Trust's infancy, it was in poor shape. Today it is splendidly restored. But the whole area along the quaysides and in Queen Street, King Street, St Margaret's Plain and Nelson Street is a treasure house of medieval industrial building that must be preserved for, as Seymour says, 'there is nothing else like it in England'. The Trust has already done much good work and seems to be winning its battle, but more remains to be done.

'Do-it-yourself' conservation in Beverley and Windsor

Beverley is another town—of Faversham's size, smaller than King's Lynn—that the tourist is apt to miss because it is tucked away in an odd corner of England, in Winifred Holtby's *South Riding* that is now part of Humberside. Like Lynn, it has two splendid churches, the two-towered Minster and the equally lovely St Mary's, and many other fine buildings. It has its own 'do-it-yourself' conservation story, or stories, for there have been several successful rescue operations performed by different groups.

One was a one-woman effort. It was the initiative of Mrs Margaret Powell, Honorary Secretary of the then East Riding branch of the CPRE, that saved the appropriately named Lady-gate, a narrow street of medieval origin leading to St Mary's church from which its name derives; a slightly run-down street of small warehouses, builders' yards, meagre shops and small houses, including some of the few medieval survivals in Beverley. By 1970, when much of the property stood empty and condemned, Mrs Powell noticed the street's potential and decided it was worthy of preservation and restoration. It seemed to her that the best way to make her point was to demonstrate what could be done with just one building. She settled on a three-storey

Georgian building, originally a malt house, that had stood empty for about seven years, persuaded the local council to lease it to her for use by the Girls Venture Corps, of which she was chairman, roped in the Young Farmers and a play group to use it as well, applied for various grants, and set to work to raise the rest of the money through the Venture Corps and Young Farmers. An architect and others gave free service, an understanding builder kept his costs down, the council, as landlord, re-roofed the building and decorated the exterior, the money was raised and the grants approved, though one of them only two days before the building was re-opened in March 1972 and the other six months later.

The building is now in daily use, but more important, other people have got the message. Other buildings in Ladygate are being restored; squalor is turning into splendour—or something not far off it—and one medieval street in one small medieval town is creeping back to life.

An even more spectacular success story of a woman's fight to save beauty from the beast has had more publicity, largely, I suspect, because the lady concerned happened to be an octogenarian, but it would still deserve attention without that admittedly piquant fact. 'Beauty' is perhaps too strong a word to use of Bachelors' Acre, an open space in the centre of Windsor, but 'beast' may not be too strong a word for the 39 'temporary' concrete garages that were erected there in 1963, and the multi-storey car park which might have been put on this land that Henry II granted to the men of Windsor in the twelfth century; nor would 'beastly' be too strong a word to apply, in this connection, to the doubtless normally estimable people who in the 1950s formed the Windsor Borough Council responsible for attempting to thwart Henry II's intentions.

That what, for want of a better term, one might call 'their knavish tricks', were defeated was mainly due to Miss Doris Mellor, a retired teacher and daughter of a former Master of Music at Eton, a lady who seems to have some of the qualities of the late Agatha Christie's Miss Marples. Miss Mellor, an outstandingly active member of the Windsor and Eton Society, having kept a keen eye on local planning matters, was not only able to warn the Society of the dangers awaiting Bachelors' Acre, but also carried on the seven-year fight to save it, which finally ended in a victory in the Court of Appeal in 1975.

There are, unfortunately, not enough Miss Mellors around and rather too many equivalents of the Windsor Borough Council, so that not every story ends so happily as the one about Bachelors' Acre, but there have been enough instances of successful conservation in recent years to give encouragement to those who fight for the cause.

Countryside rescue work

Architectural Heritage Year, 1975, produced a crop of delightful rescue jobs. Friars Quay at Norwich, for example, shows how people of moderate means can be induced to live in a city centre when a semi-derelict area is turned into a charming mixture of old and new buildings of character with a most attractive modern pub thrown in at the core of the development.

You can find other good examples of this sort of highly practical conservation in which utility goes hand in hand with the preservation—even enhancement—of attractiveness without leaving East Anglia. Two riverside projects, not unlike Friars Quay, that won conservation awards in 1974, are especially worth seeing. They are at Beccles on the Waveney, and Ely on the Cam, and both have evolved from disused maltings. The group of redbrick buildings at Beccles has been converted into eleven flats round a courtyard, and two staff flats, a restaurant and a pub round another. The malt kiln, surmounted by its pleasantly eye-catching chimney, is now the pub's main bar. The Maltings at Ely, unused since a fire in 1967, has now been converted, at no great cost, into an attractive, much needed public hall, to the astonishment of those townsfolk who saw no future for a ruined, mid-Victorian listed building and wanted it demolished and replaced by a new building.

This reversal of the Bachelors' Acre roles may surprise those people who think of town halls as invariably occupied by faceless Philistines. The fact is, however, that many local councillors, often acutely fashion-conscious, have noticed a trend away from the familiar demolish-and-replace syndrome, towards a saner policy of restoration and rehabilitation, that may yet save many town centres from becoming dead centres. Already there are examples of local authorities leading public opinion in the direction of intelligent conservation. Buckinghamshire County Council has done a splendid job in buying fine but run-down buildings in Olney, Newport Pagnell and Princes Risborough, renovating them, and then selling them, usually at a handsome profit, thus at a stroke improving the local townscapes and easing ratepayers' pockets. Suffolk Coastal District Council is embarking on a similar project in the pleasant town of Woodbridge. Swindon (now disguised as Thamesdown) Borough Council bought in 1966 the railway village that the Great Western Railway built for its workers in the 1840s, an early example of planned estate building by an industrial concern. This complex of 300 stone terrace cottages, with churches, a school, library, hospital and other public buildings is now being landscaped and improved on healthy lines, with the houses being modernised without loss of character. In one part of the estate 42 old cottages are being converted into 87 one-person homes. The council at Holywell in Clwyd has turned a once-charming row of late-Georgian, pinkish-brick cottages that had run to seed into 28 old people's flats in an alley called Panton Place now enlivened by brick and cobble paving, a seat and young trees.

These are just a few samples, taken at random, of the sort of enlightened conservation that local authorities have undertaken recently, sometimes on their own initiative, sometimes

125

after a little gentle prodding from the public. They are worth publicising to counteract the unfavourable public image that councils generally have, and, it must be admitted, often deserve.

Council success in Greater London

As few councils receive more unfavourable publicity than the Greater London Council, it is perhaps worth redressing the balance a little by pointing to their Pepys Estate by the Thames at Deptford. This was a naval victualling yard with two fine rum warehouses of 1780, two bay-windowed buildings of the same date, known as the 'superintendent's residence' and the 'office building', a Georgian coach-house, and, a short distance away, two groups of houses, one, probably by Samuel Wyatt, dating from the 1760s, the other from the 1790s. All these have not only been preserved but have been converted into ninety-three homes, a branch library and a sailing centre. Meanwhile, a more widely-publicised redevelopment scheme, the vast St Katherine's Dock project, lumbers on towards the completion date in 1985, arousing cries of delight as the splendid Ivory House warehouse of 1854 is finely restored, a mixture of cheers and groans as other more controversial buildings go up. Nobody is quite sure what the end product will look like, but at least something interesting is happening, and some handsome buildings are being preserved. But an enormous question mark still hangs over the future of other redundant docks in London and elsewhere.

The great warehouses, bonding stores and other dock buildings are among the best industrial buildings erected in the eighteenth and nineteenth centuries. None are finer than the four splendid arcaded warehouses built by Jesse Hartley to Philip Hardwick's design in Liverpool's Albert Dock in the 1840s round a space, as Tony Aldous has pointed out, twice as big as Trafalgar Square. Demolition would be tragic. A new use was projected for them, as the home of the city's Polytechnic, a magnificently imaginative piece of planning now in jeopardy.

Equally imaginative though less spectacular is the conversion of what may have been London's first riverside granary, at Rotherhithe, into a central picture reference library. The building dates from 1740 and may, if local tradition is as accurate as it so often turns out to be, contain a beam that came from the *Mayflower*, which is believed to have sailed from the site.

Such dockland buildings were usually so superbly designed and attractive to look at that their conversion to modern use almost invariably turns out well. Any doubters should go to Blakeney and see for themselves the charming flats and shops that now adorn the lower end of Ship Street in an old warehouse that when I first knew it housed the gear of fishermen and lug-worm diggers.

Canalside commitment

Canal buildings belong to the same *genre*, and there are some

126

splendid conversions up and down the country. Indeed, the reclamation of the canals in the last twenty years has been almost miraculous. Boats now glide through green pastures, and even between the scrap-yards and decaying warehouses of industrial towns, on what a decade or so ago were little more than weed-impeded trickles of water littered with the garbage of a wasteful age. All over Britain, thousands of volunteers spent their week-ends in the 1960s and 1970s bringing back to life such dead waterways as the Kennet & Avon Canal, the Caldon Canal and literally scores of others. Even as I write, I am interrupted to be told that Greater Manchester is to make a large conservation area around the famous Barton Aqueduct that carries the earliest of Britain's canals, the Bridgewater, over the Manchester Ship Canal. This swing aqueduct, built in the 1890s to replace Brindley's original stone structure, is to be at the heart of the conservation area that will include eighteenth- and nineteenth-century shops and houses around a small Georgian chapel with a strikingly elaborate Victorian graveyard, a village beyond the ship canal dominated by a Gothic church designed by E. W. Pugin in 1868, and a group of eighteenth-century farm buildings to the west surrounded by poplars; not a conventionally beautiful area, but one with the immense character that goes with canals.

46 The inmates of a local prison assisted volunteers in the restoration of this canal lock at Stratford-upon-Avon

Railway reclamation

Railways have character too, which often appeals to the same people. There is a success story to tell about the reclamation of

127

47 Saved to look out over the waters of Empingham reservoir is this classically designed church in the old county of Rutland

disused railways comparable to that of the canals. So much has been written about them that there is little need to add more here, except to mention some of those running through country that especially appeals to me, such as all those magnificent lines that climb up from the Welsh coast into the mountains; the Severn Valley line linking those lovely old rose-red towns, Bewdley and Bridgnorth; the magnificent Dart Valley line; the 'Bluebell Line' that chuffs sedately between Sheffield Park, where Edmund Gibbon used to brood about the collapse of the Roman Empire, and Horstead Keynes, carrying in 1975 a record number of passengers; finally, almost my favourite because it reminds me of childhood holidays at Whitby, the lovely, long climb up across the Yorkshire moors between Pickering and Grosmont.

One could go on recording successful pieces of restoration almost *ad infinitum*. A lovely classical church used to stand rather incongruously aloof on a grassy bank at Normanton in Rutland, looking as if it had wandered out of some London square and lost itself in the heart of the countryside. It now stands still a little incongruously and aloof, on a bank of earth and stone above the waters of the new Empingham reservoir (illustration 47), a much better place than under the waters, which was its likely fate until the conservationists got to work.

Stately home salvage

Several stately homes have been saved. Borwick Hall, a splendid

128

Tudor mansion in Lancashire, has become a county youth centre. Across the Pennines, the old palace of the Bishops of Durham at Howden, Humberside, built in 1388 when a hide-out away from that troubled border diocese was essential, has been rescued from dereliction for use as a centre for various worthwhile community projects. Winslade Manor, at Clyst St Mary, Devon, has taken on a new life as an insurance company's head office, and Witley Court in Worcestershire faces a new future after years of uncertainty since it was severely damaged by fire, at the centre of a country park.

Village victories

Whole villages have been saved from dereliction. Firwood Fold, Bolton, a hamlet of twelve cottages, including the birthplace of Samuel Crompton, the textile pioneer, is being completely restored and landscaped. Robert Owen's industrial village of New Lanark is looking forward to similar restoration. A little way to the east, the Scottish National Trust has done magnificent conservation work in the small coastal towns and villages of Fife, while Falkland in the same county, a favourite resort of James V, has become Scotland's first conservation area. In the Stour Valley on the Suffolk–Essex border, the lock that Constable painted close by his father's Flatford Mill has been restored in his bicentenary year, 1976.

On the farms there are signs that the grubbing out of hedges is nearing its end. The results of a survey published in February 1976 suggest that only 2 farmers in 10 are still planning hedge clearance, and 6 in 10 would welcome advice on conservation. Some local authorities—Staffordshire for one—offer hedgerow and tree-planting services and encourage farmers to keep field sizes below 50 acres.

Conservation conscience

Even the army now springs to attention at the mention of conservation. It is encouraging the natterjack toad to breed peacefully at Longmoor Camp in Hampshire. With the sort of publicity usually reserved for news of successful battles, it has announced that the horseshoe bat has taken up previously prepared positions in a top-secret cave somewhere in Britain.

This publicity is significant. The army, ever sensitive of its image, would not publicise its highly successful campaign for conservation if it thought there was the least risk of ridicule, or of facing that most dreaded of accusations, 'wasting the tax payers' money'. It clearly believes that public opinion now accepts conservation as being 'a good thing'.

Perhaps we ought to ask what has brought about this change of heart; what causes ordinary men, women and children to spend time and money in preserving a tidemill at Woodbridge, windmills, canals and half-forgotten railway lines all over Britain. Is it, as some people suggest, nothing more than nostalgia for days when one quarter of the earth's surface was coloured red on the globe and Britons were the international 'top people'? Have we decided to live in the past because we find the present unpleasant and the future too dreadful to contemplate?

It is a plausible theory containing an element of truth. But it does not explain all those nature reserves and nature trails that have sprung up in the last two decades. Least of all does it account for the protection of those wild wet wastelands like Borth Bog, in Wales, Rannoch Moor, in Scotland, and Wicken Fen, in England, which an American naturalist called 'England's outstanding instance of the preservation of a marshy tract for its natural beauty and historic interest'. Historic interest has nothing to do with gunboats or the road to Mandalay, and the natural beauty of wetlands has only been appreciated within the last half century. Nature conservation, it seems to me, has little to do with nostalgia. It has more to do with the present; still more with the future.

People brought up in the back streets of Black Country towns or industrial Tyneside have affection for their native hearths but want a better environment for their children. They question now if muck is inseparable from money. Some—if not yet enough— even question if economics must always have priority over beauty.

Such questioning has forced the pace of reclamation and the establishment of conservation areas, nature reserves and nature trails. Even more, it has forced the pace of those living museums, especially open-air museums (see Appendix 1), that are rapidly replacing those old museums which, to quote Dylan Thomas, 'ought to be in a museum'. Only the direst of economic circumstances can prevent that pace from increasing, because the need for them is urgent, largely because the public generally lack confidence in their own judgement of what is beautiful or historically interesting. They will drive to Pretty Corner, near Sheringham, because the name suggests that the effort will be worthwhile—and for the more sceptical there is a notice-board telling them that it is a beauty spot—but they will drive unheeding past many prettier corners if there are no other people there admiring the view. So once you label a place a conservation area or a nature reserve, you get swarms of visitors eager to see what they are assured is worth seeing. They will stand and admire buildings re-erected in open air museums that they may have ignored when the buildings stood on their original sites.

But we do not want the whole country to become a living museum; a country which foreigners visit merely to gaze at the past. Conservationists are sometimes accused, not always unfairly, of wanting to preserve everything more than a century old, or even less. That sort of automatic protest against all change is self-defeating because it raises accusations of crankiness and weakens the many strong cases. Admittedly, there are borderline examples, like the vast derelict flour mill of 1898 on the banks of the Tawe at Swansea. It seems to me to be monstrously ugly but, as reputable bodies like the Victorian Society point out, it was the first multi-storey reinforced-concrete frame building in Britain, possibly in Europe, and therefore should be saved.

This is a difficult one, but usually the best hope for the future lies in the sort of sensible, imaginative development that preserves the best of the past and blends it with good modern planning on the lines of the Friars Quay and other projects mentioned in this chapter, together with an acceleration of the sort of reclamation of derelict land that is going on at Stoke and elsewhere. What we must avoid is finding ourselves living in a country of vast concrete jungles interspersed wtih fossilised 'olde worlde' villages and artificially preserved 'natural' countryside.

How can we avoid it? Ideally, by developing the sort of taste the Georgians had that enabled them to put every brick, plant and tree to the best possible advantage. Since that is beyond reasonable expectation, the next best hope lies in educating first the public and then the government. The best way we can do that is by joining organisations like the CPRE, the numerous county naturalists' trusts, historic buildings' trusts, civic societies and the various other bodies seeking to preserve the best of Britain and to make the best use of our still-considerable resources of natural and man-made beauty. Individually our voices do not carry far. Collectively, they can echo down the corridors of power until the authorities have to listen.

Those authorities, the mysterious 'they', ought, in a democracy, to be 'us'. If we can convince them of that—and there are signs of it happening—what remains of the best of Britain may yet be saved. But time is not on our side. While much derelict land is being cleared, new areas are being laid waste at about the same rate. For every good building saved, another is lost. Britain is still vanishing. It is only the rate of disapperance that may be slowing down. There is still too much that needs to be seen now. Tomorrow may be too late.

Appendices

Appendix 1 Some Living Museums

There are more than 900 museums in Britain. This is just a very small personal selection of living museums, by which I mean museums where the exhibits are not all confined to glass cases. Some might have been more justly described as working museums because some at least of the exhibits are active. I have included several open-air museums. For a full list, and for opening times, see the annual *Museums and Galleries Guide*, or the AA's *Britain's Heritage*.

ENGLAND

Avon Bristol. SS *Great Britain*. In the floating dock in which she was built in 1844, off Cumberland Road, Isambard Kingdom Brunel's great iron ship is being restored after an ill-fated career

Derbyshire Crich Tramway Museum. Rides in tramcars recovered from cities in various parts of the world, amid nostalgic Edwardian advertisements in a quarry worked by George Stephenson

Devon Morwellham. Not so much a museum, more a forgotten riverside port now being restored; Exeter Maritime Museum. Town Quay and Canal Basin. Around 50 old sail and steam vessels, old warehouses and oldest canal pound lock in England

Durham Beamish, nr Stanley. North of England Open Air Museum. Opened in 1972 as Britain's first open-air museum 'where people can look into the past and see how things worked', it is gradually covering its 270-acre site with relics of the area's industries

Gloucestershire Guiting Power. Cotswold Farm Park. Rare breeds of farmyard animals

Hereford and Worcester Stoke Prior, nr Bromsgrove. Avoncroft Museum of Buildings. Reconstructed houses and a windmill

Lancashire Haslingden. Higher Mill, Helmshore. Late-eighteenth-century fulling mill now being converted into a textile museum

Lincolnshire Burgh-le-Marsh. Five-sail tower windmill in working order, with small local history collection

London National Maritime Museum, Greenwich. A must

Norfolk Cockley Cley. Two remarkable museums in tiny village. Reconstruction of Iceni settlement on original site, with the local story brought up to present day in nearby cottage dating from 1450; Norwich. Bridewell Museum of Local Industries and Rural Crafts housed in fourteenth-century merchant's house, used later as a prison Also, Stranger's Hall. Another fourteenth-century

132

merchant's house. Rooms show history of furnishing tastes from Tudor to Victorian times

Northamptonshire Stoke Bruerne. Waterways Museum. Splendid collection of canalania in former corn mill alongside Grand Union Canal

Nottinghamshire Lound Hall, near Retford. Small but interesting coal-mining museum; Papplewick. Pumping House. Impressive beam engines in cathedral-like atmosphere

Shropshire Telford. Ironbridge Gorge Museum. 'A sort of national park of industrial archaeology'. Essential viewing

South Yorkshire Sheffield. Abbeydale Industrial Hamlet. Late-eighteenth-century scythe works and dependent settlement, typical of the infant Sheffield-steel industry

Staffordshire Cheddleton. Flint mill in wooded surroundings on River Churnet. Stoke-on-Trent. Gladstone Pottery Museum, Longton

Suffolk Saxted Green, near Framlingham. Late-eighteenth-century post windmill. Stowmarket. Abbot's Hall Museum of Rural Life in East Anglia

Sussex Singleton. Weald and Downland Open Air Museum. Restored buildings include fourteenth-century farmhouse, sixteenth-century treadmill and nineteenth-century toll-house

Tyne and Wear Monkwearmouth Railway Station. Impressive station of 1848, now housing growing transport museum

Wiltshire Crofton, near Devizes. Pumping station including two massive beam engines above a staircase of twenty-nine locks on Kennet & Avon Canal

York Railway Museum. Recently reopened

ISLE OF MAN

Cregneash Manx Village Folk Museum. Thatched cottages preserved include workshops of a turner, weaver, crofter and smith

Laxey Giant waterwheel built to pump water from lead-mines in 1854 now restored to working order

NORTHERN IRELAND

Belfast Ulster Folk Museum, Craigavad. Nineteenth-century water-powered spademill, among other reconstructed buildings

SCOTLAND

East Lothian East Linton. Preston Mill, Prestonkirk. Seventeenth-century corn mill restored to full working order and owned by National Trust for Scotland

Inverness-shire Kingussie. Highland Folk Museum. A clack mill, among several other reconstructed buildings

WALES

Gwynedd Blaenau Ffestiniog. Llechwedd slate caverns. Railway trips to working slate face; Llanberis. North Wales Quarrying Museum housed in original workshops of Dinorwic quarries

South Glamorgan St Fagans. Welsh Folk Museum. Reconstructed farmhouses, a tannery, working woollen mill, tollhouse and lots more

Appendix 2 Looking for Crafts and Craftsmen

You may have to search diligently to find the old crafts practised. Some are vanishing as the older generation of craftsmen fade away. Two of these craftsmen who I happen to know have recently retired. Herbert Marrison is one. The last of a long line of rope-makers who worked the rope walk at the entrance to Peak Cavern, Castleton, Derbyshire, for 400 years, he was still prepared to oblige a neighbour by making a strong clothes line in his spare time until his ninetieth birthday. Now he is living in retirement in the south of England, but his rope walk can still be seen at Castleton. George Higginson of Berkswell in Warwickshire laid what he claims to be the last hedge in June 1976 after 40 years of hedge-laying. In these days there is more demand for people who can grub up hedges than for those who can lay new ones.

It is the uncertainty about the future that discourages young men from taking up these crafts. Few boys and girls leaving school are willing to risk learning a trade that may die, they think, long before they reach retiring age. Farriers tell me that there is no shortage of work for them, but there is a shortage of young people prepared to learn a craft which they believe may have a limited future. It is rather the same with thatching. My impression is that the demand for thatchers is growing rather than declining, but the youngsters tend not to see it that way. It is a trade that most young men reject, perhaps not unnaturally, because of its 'olde worlde' image, out of keeping with their dream world of gleaming motor bikes and glistening girls. Another more pertinent reason may be that the work involves long spells of work away from home. George Mellor of Cromford, at the southern end of the Peak District, has three assistant thatchers working for him, but much of their work lies outside their home area with its traditional stone slate roofs.

48 Luckily, the craft of the stone-waller survives. This one is at work in Cornwall. The soil infill will eventually grow vegetation to produce the typical Cornish 'hedge'

On the whole, it is the slightly older generation who take up the old crafts, having found the modern production line unsatisfying and the pace of the 'rat race' displeasing. In the Lake District, the Cotswolds, the Highlands of Scotland and North Wales you will find men—and sometimes women—working longer hours for less pay than they earned in the cities, turning out from small workshops handsome articles in wood, wrought iron or almost any other material you can name for the sheer joy that creativity brings. Apart from the satisfaction that this work brings to themselves, and to their customers, these people are helping to keep alive the old crafts.

Where can one find these craftsmen and their workshops? The best starting point is the Council for Small Industries in Rural Areas (CoSIRA), 35 Camp Road, Wimbledon Common, London SW19, which will provide details on where to see rural craftsmen, museums and collections. They publish an excellent CoSIRA Guide to Country Workshops in Britain (50p, at present) which lists over a thousand places where visitors are welcome.

Several of the Living Museums mentioned in Appendix 1 have splendid displays of country crafts. The Welsh Folk Museum at St Fagan's is excellent. The museum of English Rural Life at the University of Reading is another that should not be missed. The Open-air Museums at Singleton in Sussex, Stowmarket and Avoncroft, near Bromsgrove, are good on rural crafts, as are two in Yorkshire, the Ryedale Folk Museum, at Hutton-le-Hole, near Pickering, and the West Yorkshire Folk Museum, Shibden Hall, Halifax. The York Castle Museum and Norwich Bridewell have interesting collections, as have Hartlebury Castle, near Kidderminster, and Bicton Gardens, just north of Budleigh Salterton in Devon. Shughborough Hall, Staffordshire, has a growing collection, and there is a small but interesting collection of farm carts and caravans at the Elvaston Castle Country Park, near Derby.

Demonstrations of such old woodland crafts as pit sawing and wood turning can be seen at the Forestry Commission's Mayswood Centre near Warwick, and visitors to Hardwick Hall in Derbyshire, until the year 1980 at least, will be able to observe craftsmen in wood and stone working on a large scale restoration of the house that has already been in progress for more than five years, so intricate is the work and so thorough the workers.

The age of craftsmanship, indeed, is not dead. The masons permanently employed at Chatsworth are every bit as good, says the Duchess of Devonshire, as those who built the present mansion between 1685 and 1707. In less exalted places, you may find further evidence of this high standard, especially in the stone belts where men still make walls that will stand up for half a century or more against everything but the deliberate vandalism of those who remove stones to enrich their suburban garden rockeries. There are still full-time stonewallers, though their numbers are unfortunately decreasing, and you may be lucky enough to see some at work, as Frank Rodgers was between Veryon and Tregoney in Cornwall (see page 134). Demonstrations are sometimes given at agricultural shows and the increasingly popular farm 'open days'.

Indeed, it pays to keep an eye on local newspapers for demonstrations such as these and such exhibitions of local crafts as are held each summer in places as widely separated as Criccieth and Blakeney, and probably in many more in between. It pays, too, to keep one's eye open along the roads of rural England and to make inquiries about local crafts in country pubs and shops. You may even be as lucky as Anthony Richardson who, while learning his part in *Hamlet* at Stratford-upon-Avon, encountered two hedge-

135

layers while out for a walk. He asked what their particular jobs were. 'Well,' said one, 'I shapes the ends, and he rough hews them.' Thus came to life for Richardson one piece of Shakespearean imagery, together with the sudden realisation that Shakespeare's England is not all that far away from our own. Nowhere are they closer together than in the craftsman's workshop.

Appendix 3 Useful Addresses of Conservation Bodies

Ancient Monuments Society
Secretary: 33 Ladbroke Square, London W11
Association for Industrial Archaeology
Secretary: Church Hill, Ironbridge, Telford, Salop TF8 7RE
Association for Protection of Rural Scotland
20 Falkland Avenue, Newton Mearns, Renfrewshire
Central Council for Rivers Protection
Fishmongers' Hall, London EC4
Centre for Environmental Studies
5 Cambridge Terrace, London NW1
The Civic Trust
17 Carlton House Terrace, London SW1
Civic Trust for Scotland
24 George Square, Glasgow C2
Civic Trust for Wales
Snelling House, Bute Terrace, Cardiff
Civic Trust for the North East
34 Saddler Street, Durham
Civic Trust for the North West
56 Oxford Street, Manchester 1
Coastal Anti-Pollution League
'Alverstoke', Greenway Lane, Bath, Somerset
Committee for Environmental Conservation (CoEnCo)
4 Hobart Place, London EC4
Commons, Open Spaces and Footpaths Preservation Society
Suite 4, 166 Shaftesbury Avenue, London WC2
Conservation Society
12 London Street, Chertsey, Surrey
Council for Environmental Education
26 Bedford Square, London WC1
Council for Nature
Zoological Gardens, Regent's Park, London NW1
Council for the Protection of Rural England (CPRE)
4 Hobart Place, London SW1W 0HY
Council for the Protection of Rural Wales
Meifod, Montgomeryshire
Council for Places of Worship (formerly *Council for the Care of Churches*)
83 London Wall, London EC2
Country Landowners' Association
16 Belgrave Square, London SW1
Countryside Commission
John Dower House, Crescent Place, Cheltenham, Glos
Countryside Commission for Scotland
Battleby, Redgorton, Perth
Fauna Preservation Society
c/o Zoological Society of London, Regent's Park, London NW1
Field Studies Council
9 Devereux Court, London WC2
Friends of the Earth (FOE), UK
8 King Street, London WC2

Georgian Group
2 Chester Street, London SW1
Inland Waterways Association
114 Regent's Park Road, London NW1
Keep Britain Tidy Group
Bostel House, 37 West Street, Brighton, Sussex
Landmark Trust
43 Cloth Fair, London EC4
Men of the Trees
Crawley Down, Crawley, Sussex
National Society for Clean Air
136 North Street, Brighton, Sussex
National Trust for places of Historic Interest or Natural Beauty
42 Queen Anne's Gate, London SW1
National Trust for Scotland for places of Historic Interest or Natural Beauty
5 Charlotte Square, Edinburgh 2
Nature Conservancy Council
19 Belgrave Square, London SW1
Noise Abatement Society
6 Old Bond Street, London W1
Ramblers' Association
1–4 Crawford Mews, York Street, London W1
Redundant Churches Fund
St Andrew-by-the-Wardrobe, Queen Victoria Street, London EC4
Royal Forestry Society of England, Wales and Northern Ireland
102 High Street, Tring, Hertfordshire
Royal Scottish Forestry Society
Drumsheuth Gardens, Edinburgh
Royal Society for the Protection of Birds
The Lodge, Sandy, Beds
Save Britain's Heritage
6A Bedford Square, London WC1
Save the Village Pond Campaign
British Waterfowl Association, The Rectory, Birchanger, Bishop's Stortford, Herts
Scottish Society for the Protection of Wild Birds
125 Douglas Street, Glasgow
Soil Association
Walnut Tree Manor, Haughley, Stowmarket, Suffolk
Society for the Promotion of Nature Conservation
The Green, Nettleham, Lincs
Society for the Protection of Ancient Buildings
55 Great Ormond Street, London WC1
Town and Country Planning Association
17 Carlton House Terrace, London SW1
Victorian Society
1 Priory Gardens, Bedford Park, London W4
World Wildlife Fund
7–8 Plumtree Court, London EC4

Most English and Welsh counties have Archaeological Societies, as have several Scottish counties. A list of these can be found in *Whitaker's Almanack*. Several counties have Historic Buildings Trusts which are concerned to preserve ancient buildings in their areas. Most have Naturalists' Trusts. Many towns and some villages have organisations concerned with preserving the beauties and historic interest of their localities. The appropriate county library will be able to supply the addresses of the secretaries of these bodies.

Bibliography

Extensive use has been made of the publications issued by many of the bodies listed in Appendix 3. The annual report and bi-monthly bulletins of the CPRE have been especially helpful, as has *Conservation Review*, issued quarterly by the *Society for the Promotion of Nature Conservation* and circulated free to members of county naturalists' trusts. The publications of the various national park authorities, such as the quarterly *Peak Park News*, and such amenity bodies as the Friends of the Lake District, The Exmoor Society and the Dartmoor Preservation Association have yielded much useful material, as have such periodicals as *Architectural Review, Country Life, The Countryman* and *Town and Country Planning*. Newspapers like the *Guardian, Times, Sunday Times* and *Observer* nowadays devote much space to conservation and related topics and, along with numerous local weekly papers and some county magazines have signposted trails that have been well worth following.

Chapter 1
Arvill, Robert. *Man and Environment* (Penguin, 1967)
Fairbrother, Nan. *New Lives, New Landscapes* (The Architectural Press, 1970)
Kennet, Wayland. *Preservation* (Temple Smith, 1972)
Smith, Anthony. *Beside the Seaside* (George Allen & Unwin, 1972)
Steers, J. A. *The English Coast* (Collins, 1966)

Chapter 2
Aldous, Tony. *Battle for the Environment* (Collins/Fontana, 1972)
Borrow, George. *Wild Wales* (Dent/Everyman, ND originally published 1862)
Christian, Roy. *The Peak District* (David & Charles, 1975)
Bonham-Carter, Victor. *Survival of the English Countryside* (Hodder & Stoughton, 1971)
Brandon, Peter. *The Sussex Landscape* (Hodder & Stoughton, 1973)
Condry, W. M. *Snowdonia* (Collins, New Naturalist Series, 1966)
Emery, Frank. *The Oxfordshire Landscape* (Hodder & Stoughton, 1974)
Gill, Crispin (ed). *Dartmoor, A New Study* (David & Charles, 1970)
Gregory, Roy. *The Price of Amenity* (Macmillan, 1971)
Hoskin, W. G. *The Making of the English Landscape* (Hodder & Stoughton, 1955)
Kimber, R. & Richardson, J. S. (eds). *Campaign for the Environment* (Routledge & Kegan Paul, 1974)

Steane, John M. *The Northamptonshire Landscape* (Hodder & Stoughton, 1974)

Chapter 3
Arvill, Robert. *Man and Environment* (Penguin, 1967)
Burrows, R. *Naturalist in Devon & Cornwall* (David & Charles, 1971)
Carson, R. *Silent Spring* (Hamish Hamilton, 1963)
Christian, Garth. *A Place for Animals* (Lutterworth Press, 1958)
——. *Tomorrow's Countryside* (John Murray, 1966)
Condry, W. M. *Snowdonia* (Collins, New Naturalist Series, 1966)
Hardy, Eric. *Naturalist in Lakeland* (David & Charles, 1973)
Knowlton, Derrick. *Naturalist in Scotland* (David & Charles, 1974)
Leutscher, Alfred. *Epping Forest* (David & Charles, 1974)
Lockley, R. M. *Naturalist in Wales* (David & Charles, 1970)
Mabey, Richard. *The Roadside Wildlife Book* (David & Charles, 1974)
Mellanby, K. *Pesticides and Pollution* (Collins, 1967)
Pollard, E., Hooper, M. D., & Moore, M. W. *Hedges* (Collins, New Naturalist Series, 1974)
Stamp, J. D. *Nature Conservation in Britain* (Collins, 1969)
Vesey-Fitzgerald, Brian. *The Vanishing Wildlife of Britain* (Macgibbon & Kee, 1969)

Chapter 4
Christian, Garth. *Tomorrow's Countryside* (John Murray, 1966)
Lindley, Kenneth. *Coastline* (Hutchinson, 1967)
——. *Seaside Architecture* (Hugh Evelyn, 1972)
Manning-Saunders, Ruth. *Seaside England* (Batsford, 1951)
Pimlott, J. A. R. *Englishman's Holiday* (Faber & Faber, 1947)
Smith, Anthony. *Beside the Seaside* (George Allen & Unwin, 1972)

Chapter 5
Aldous, Tony. *Good-bye Britain* (Sidgwick & Jackson, 1975)
Buchanan, C. D. *Traffic in Towns* (Penguin, 1964)
Cullen, G. *Townscape* (Architectural Press, 1961)
Fairbrother, Nan. *New Lives, New Landscapes* (Architectural Press, 1970)
Ferguson, Adam. *The Sack of Bath* (Compton Russell, 1973)
Pevsner, Sir Nikolaus. All the books in the *Buildings of England* series (Penguin)

Chapter 6
Beresford, M. W. *The Lost Villages of England* (Lutterworth Press, 1954)
Blythe, Ronald. *Akenfield* (Allen Lane, The Penguin Press, 1969)
Bonham-Carter, Victor. *The English Village* (Penguin, 1952)
Burke, John. *English Villages* (Batsford, 1975)
Hoskins, W. G. *The Making of the English Landscape* (Hodder & Stoughton, 1955)
Jennings, Paul. *The Living Village* (Hodder & Stoughton, 1968)
Tate, W. E. *The English Village Community* (Gollancz, 1967)
Thompson, Flora. *Lark Rise to Candleford* (Oxford University Press, 1959)

Chapter 7
Aldous, Tony. *Good-bye Britain* (Sidgwick & Jackson, 1975)
Barman, Christian. *Introduction to Railway Architecture* (Penguin, 1950)

Pevsner, Sir Nikolaus. All the books in the *Buildings of England* series (Penguin)

Strong, Roy, Binney, Marcus & Harris, John. *The Destruction of the Country House* (Thames & Hudson, 1974)

Chapter 8

Arvill, Robert. *Man and Environment* (Penguin, 1967)

Barr, John. *Derelict Britain* (Penguin, 1969)

Christian, Garth. *Tomorrow's Countryside* (John Murray, 1967)

Crowe, Sylvia. *Tomorrow's Landscape* (Architectural Press, 1956)

Fairbrother, Nan. *New Lives, New Landscapes* (Architectural Press, 1970)

——. *The Nature of Landscape Design* (Architectural Press, 1974)

Mabey, Richard. *The Unofficial Countryside* (Collins, 1973)

140

Acknowledgements

I am grateful to the many people who have helped me to collect the material for this book. I would particularly like to thank Dr W. I. Stanton for so kindly allowing me to use certain passages from his paper on quarrying, which appeared in *Man and the Mendips*, produced by the Mendip Society in 1971. My debt to the CPRE is considerable, and I especially want to thank Mr Christopher Hall, Director, not only for so kindly writing the Foreword but also for his ready help in checking certain information; Mr John Yeoman, sometime Assistant Secretary, for drawing my attention to several particularly acute dangers to the environment; Lt Col R. A. Fell, TD, Honorary Secretary of the Northamptonshire Branch; Mr C. R. Nicholls, FCIS, FCCA, Honorary Secretary of the Shropshire Branch, and Mr E. H. Smith, Assistant Secretary of the Essex Branch, for the immense trouble they went to in clearing up several points. I am similarly indebted to Mrs Mamie Turner, General Secretary of the Gloucester Civic Trust, and Mr John Popham, FRICS, Director of the Suffolk Preservation Society, for so kindly answering my questions.

Grateful acknowledgement must be made for permission to use photographs to Mr Frank Rodgers, as so often in the past, John Martin (Staffordshire) Ltd, and the Corporation of Stoke-on-Trent, and Mr Geoffrey N. Wright.

Finally, I must thank Mrs Pat Paling for her remarkably speedy and accurate typing; Miss Emma Wood, of David & Charles, who not only suggested the idea of the book but also became its immensely patient midwife; and my wife who, during the research for and writing of *Vanishing Britain*, had to put up with—or more accurately, without—a frequently vanishing husband.

Index

Page numbers in italic type refer to illustrations

142